❧

VIRAGO
CLASSIC NON-FICTION

Isabella Bird

Isabella Lucy Bird (1831–1904), the daughter of a clergy-man, grew up in Tattenhall, Cheshire. Early in life she suffered from a spinal complaint and in 1854 she was sent by her doctor to America and Canada to improve her health. She continued to suffer from back trouble, insomnia and depression until, at the age of forty, she set off for Australia and Hawaii where her health miraculously improved. She wrote *Six Months in the Sandwich Islands* (1875) and climbed the world's largest volcano. In 1873, Isabella Bird set off for the Rocky Mountains; her letters were published in *Leisure Hour* in 1878 and later published in this edition in 1879. In 1881 Isabella married Dr John Bishop, who died in 1886. Other journeys led to *Unbeaten Tracks in Japan* (1880), *The Golden Chersonese* (1885), *Journeys in Persia and Kurdistan* (1891), *Among the Tibetans* (1894), *Korea and Her Neighbours* (1898) and *The Yangtze Valley and Beyond* (1899).

Isabella Bird died in Edinburgh in 1904.

A LADY'S LIFE
IN THE
ROCKY MOUNTAINS

Isabella L. Bird

With an Introduction by Pat Barr

A *Virago* Book

Published by VIRAGO PRESS 1982

Reprinted 1991, 1996

First published in Great Britain by John Murray 1879

Introduction copyright © Pat Barr 1982

The moral right of the author has been asserted.

All rights reserved.
No part of this publication may be reproduced,
stored in a retrieval system, or transmitted, in any
form or by any means, without the prior
permission in writing of the publisher, nor be
otherwise circulated in any form of binding or
cover other than that in which it is published and
without a similar condition including this
condition being imposed on the subsequent purchaser.

A CIP catalogue record for this book
is available from the British Library.

ISBN 0 86068 267 6

Printed in England by Clays Ltd, St Ives plc

UK companies, institutions and other organisations wishing
to make bulk purchases of this or any other books
published by Little, Brown, should contact their local
bookshop or the special sales department at the address below.
Tel 0171 911 8000. Fax 0171 911 8100.

Virago
A Division of
Little, Brown and Company (UK)
Brettenham House
Lancaster Place
London WC2E 7EN

TO MY SISTER,

TO WHOM

THESE LETTERS WERE ORIGINALLY WRITTEN,

THEY ARE NOW

AFFECTIONATELY DEDICATED.

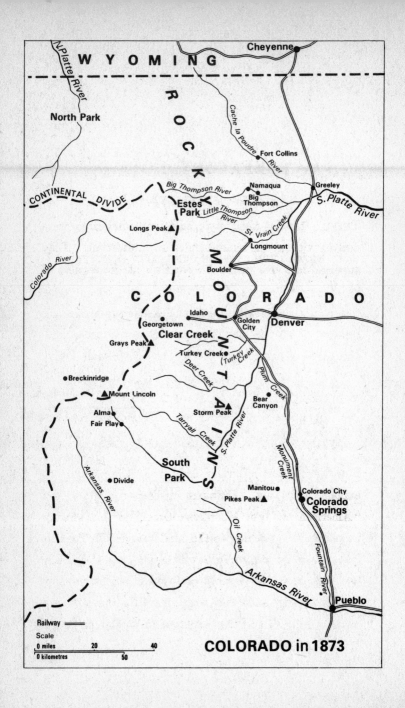

COLORADO in 1873

Railway ——

Scale

0 miles   20   40

0 kilometres   50

WYOMING

N.Platte River

North Park

Cheyenne

ROCKY

Cache la Poudre River

Fort Collins

CONTINENTAL DIVIDE

Big Thompson River

Namaqua

Greeley

Estes Park

Little Thompson River

Big Thompson

S. Platte River

Longs Peak ▲

St Vrain Creek

Longmount

Colorado River

Boulder

COLORADO

MOUNTAINS

Idaho

Golden City

Denver

Georgetown

Clear Creek

Grays Peak ▲

Turkey Creek

(Turkey Creek)

Breckinridge

Deer Creek

▲ Mount Lincoln

Storm Peak ▲

Bear Canyon

Alma

Plum Creek

Fair Play

Tarryall Creek

S. Platte River

South Park

Monument Creek

Divide

Manitou

Colorado City

Pikes Peak ▲

Colorado Springs

Arkansas River

Oil Creek

Fountain River

Arkansas River

Pueblo

PREFATORY NOTE.

————♦————

THESE letters, as their style sufficiently indicates, were
written without the remotest idea of publication. They
appeared last year in the *Leisure Hour* at the request of
its editor, and were so favourably received that I venture to present them to the public in a separate form, as
a record of very interesting travelling experiences, and
of a phase of pioneer life which is rapidly passing away.

October 21, 1879.   I. L. B.

NOTE TO SECOND EDITION.

FOR the benefit of other lady travellers, I wish to
explain that my "Hawaiian riding dress" is the
"American Lady's Mountain Dress," a half-fitting
jacket, a skirt reaching to the ankles, and full Turkish
trousers gathered into frills which fall over the boots,
—a thoroughly serviceable and feminine costume for
mountaineering and other rough travelling in any part
of the world. I add this explanation to the prefatory

note, together with a rough sketch of the costume,[1] in consequence of an erroneous statement[2] in the *Times* of November 22d.   I. L. B.

November 27, 1879.

NOTE TO THIRD EDITION.

IN consequence of the accidental omission of the date of my sojourn in the Rocky Mountains having been pointed out to me, I take this opportunity of stating that I was there in the autumn and early winter of 1873, on my way back to England from the Sandwich Islands. The Letters are a faithful picture of the country and manner of living six years ago ; but I learn from friends who have travelled in Colorado during the last six months, that the prediction in the note on page 121 is being rapidly fulfilled, that log cabins are fast giving place to frame houses, and that the footprints of elk and big-horn may be searched for in vain on the dewy grass of Estes Park.   I. L. B.

EDINBURGH, *January* 16, 1880.

[1] See *Title-page.*
[2] "She donned masculine habiliments for greater convenience."

TABLE OF CONTENTS.

XI.

XII.

XIII.

XIV.

XV.

INTRODUCTION

———◆———

"Isabella Bird is the ideal traveller," wrote the
Spectator critic in 1879, when the first edition of *A
Lady's Life in the Rocky Mountains* appeared. "There
never was anybody who had adventures as well as
Miss Bird." And, considering the splendid outcrop of
dauntless and extraordinary Victorian travellers,
this was no mean praise. Isabella Bird was intrepid,
observant, energetic, inquisitive, hardy, intelligent,
unassuming, resourceful; she thrived on the rigours
of nineteenth-century travel; she adapted easily and
cheerfully to strangers and unfamiliar environments;
she wrote with perceptive honesty about her
astonishing journeys in many far-flung parts of the
world. In short, the *Spectator's* verdict was justified.

The single most curious aspect of Isabella's curious
life is that a woman of her background, upbringing
and physique managed to accomplish what she did.
Initially, she did not have a great deal going for her;
but very few women in Victorian times went so far.
Born in 1831, elder daughter of Edward Bird, an
English clergyman related to the famous Wilberforce
family, she grew up in an atmosphere of high-
mindedness, earnest study and worthy causes. But

she was dogged by ill-health, and spent much of her youth reclining in various chilly rectory parlours suffering from incipient spinal disease and the 'nervous debility' common among intelligent, high-spirited girls of the period, who were thwarted by lack of formal education and oppressed by constrictive social conventions. Her closest companion at this time, who became the centre of her emotional life, was her younger sister Henrietta, who possessed the traditionally "feminine" qualities of natural piety, docility and gentleness of spirit that Isabella conspicuously lacked.

In 1854, when Isabella was twenty-three, a perceptive doctor prescribed a long sea voyage to cure her various maladies and she took off to America, Canada – and her first taste of freedom. The freshness and vigour of the transatlantic scene immediately exhilarated her and her first book, *An Englishwoman in America*, published in decorous anonymity, clearly suggests both a capacity for zestful adventure and an ability to write vividly about it. Soon after her return, however, her beloved father died, and during the 1860s, she, her mother and sister led the staid, dutiful lives typical of such middle-class gentlewomen. Even in those convention-ridden circumstances Isabella couldn't run quite true to form; she made several trips to the wild Outer Hebrides, and wrote articles about the sorry plight of the island crofters that helped arouse public sympathy for their cause. But this was small beer for one of Isabella's capacity. She continued to suffer from insomnia, back trouble and depression until, in 1872 at the age of forty, she took off for the very Antipodes in a mood of kill-or-cure desperation.

She found Australia totally uncongenial and disappointing, and soon set sail again for the Sandwich Isles (now Hawaii) where the miracle first happened: almost as soon as she landed on those lush, carefree islands her lassitude, low spirits, aches and pains simply vanished. The dumpily-built, earnest, sickly clergyman's daughter was metamorphosed into a traveller of boundless energy, enthusiasm and derring-do. While there, she "rioted most luxuriantly" in the "congenial life of the wilds", she wrote to Henrietta; she slept in native grass-huts, went bullock-hunting with the cattle-men and became the second known white woman to scale the 13,650 feet high Mauna Loa, the world's largest volcano, the 'Matterhorn of the Pacific'.

It was this newly-fledged, newly-fired lady who, after leaving Honolulu, reached the Rocky Mountains in the autumn of 1873. At that time Colorado, where she stayed longest, was an untamed territory outside the Union, its laws and railroads in the process of being laid down, its virgin lands inhabited by hard-living, hard-drinking pioneer settlers who had only recently and brutally seized them from the Indians. Estes Park, the apogee and apotheosis of Isabella's Rocky Mountain experience, and now a popular, easily-accessible tourist resort, was then the beautiful, isolated wilderness she so rapturously describes. As for Rocky Mountain Jim, the free-

lancing, freeloading stock-raiser and trapper who
nearly ensnared her heart – he and his kind would
soon be as rare as the mountain lions prowling there,
in territories soon to be tamed by the advances of
'modern progress'.

The surprisingly intense relationship that developed between Isabella and her "dear desperado",
as she called Jim Nugent, was as improbable as any
musical comedy plot, and more fascinating because,
as far as one can judge from material still extant, it
was the nearest Isabella ever came in her life to a
romantic sexual passion. It is evident from her
descriptions of their early encounters that she was
quickly won over by the heady combination of Jim's
handsome physique, chivalrous manner, "refined"
accent, theatrical flair – and dangerously violent
reputation. Clearly too, the unlikely attraction was
mutual.

In fact, the relationship went rather further than
the published account of it suggests, for Isabella
edited out a few deeply-felt passages on the subject
that she wrote home for Henrietta's eyes only. In one
of them, she says Jim confessed that ". . . as soon as I
had gone away [on her horseback expedition through
the territory] he had discovered that he was attached
to me and it was killing him . . . I was terrified. It
made me shake all over and even cry. He is a man
any woman might love, but no sane woman would
marry." Nor, she adds hastily, ". . . did he ask me to
marry him."

Nevertheless, Jim was determined to entrammel

her untried emotions as long as possible, and it was following this declaration of his affection that he, ". . . in a rush of wild eloquence that was truly thrilling" (Letter xiv) told her the full and doubtlessly much embellished story of his "desperado's career". "He is so lovable and yet so terrible," she explained to Henrietta, in extenuation of her bewitchment. Days later, when he became "ill" and she galloped to his cabin (Letter xv), she told him that, "If all circumstances on both sides had been favourable and I had loved him with my whole heart, I would not dare to trust my happiness to him because of the whisky . . . He said he would never say another word of love." Soon after that, sensible Isabella, though still much attracted by this flamboyant man "with two faces", managed to put aside the fearful prospect of "love" and tear herself away from Estes Park.

The following year, as she mentions in a footnote (Letter xvii), Jim Nugent was shot by cheery Griff Evans in a fracas, the full truth of which was never revealed. Jim himself lived long enough after the attack to claim he was shot because he refused to sell his squatter's land to Lord Dunraven, whose agent Mr Haigh (Mr Fodder in the Letters) Isabella introduced to him as she was leaving. This explains her rather cryptic footnote in Letter xvii; what remains unexplained is the precise degree of emotional involvement that Isabella and Jim shared for a brief period. But at least and mercifully Isabella had the strength to reject the romantic dream of an almost-literal "shacking up" with her "dear desperado", which, given their totally disparate temperaments and backgrounds, would surely have ended disastrously. Instead, a little glum, she returned to the calm security of sister Henrietta and a boating holiday on the River Ouse.

For Isabella Bird had a great deal more to do with her life than nurse the vanities and tantrums of Jim Nugent, and the first task was properly to establish herself as a writer of first-rate travel books. In 1875, her *Six Months in the Sandwich Isles* was published by John Murray, who remained her life-long friend and counsellor as well as publisher. The book was well received by the critics and this encouraged her to work on her American material, which first appeared serially in the genteel weekly, *Leisure Hour*, in 1878, entitled *Letters from the Rocky Mountains*. The book form appeared the following year, as did the first American edition by G. P. Putnam Sons of New York. It received rave notices on both sides of the Atlantic for its lively candour, its vivid detailing of the natural world and an "unadorned narrative" which, claimed the *Spectator*, was " . . . of more interest than most novels".

The most "novelettish" aspect of Isabella's expedition had been carefully expurgated of course so that, to her relief, not one critic "scented out any imagined impropriety". Not, at least, in relation to Jim Nugent, but *The Times* reviewer commented that Miss Bird ". . . donned masculine habiliments for her greater convenience" when on horseback.

Isabella was absolutely furious, and apparently suggested to John Murray that, as she was a properly-clad lady who never, ever wore "masculine habilments" or in any way aspired to man's estate, he might like to thrash *The Times*' editor on her behalf? This he declined to do, and Isabella was mollified eventually by the sketch of herself in a feminine-looking riding dress, "such as is worn by *ladies* in Hawaii and America", that appeared in most subsequent editions of the book. It ran to eight editions in all, the last by Putnams in 1912; long before that, Isabella Bird was thoroughly established among the most celebrated and accomplished writer-travellers of her day.

Following her adventures in the Rocky Mountains and the publication of the two books, Isabella's health and spirits again deteriorated in the lacklustre landscapes of "dear Home" and again she fled to wilder climes – to the northern Japanese island of Hokkaido and the Native States of Malaya (the latter journey resulting in her splendidly rich *The Golden Chersonese*). In 1880 she faced the greatest emotional test of her life when her beloved sister Henrietta died of typhoid. "She is not – and the light, life and inspiration of my life have died with her", she wrote to a friend. It must have been partly on the rebound that the following year she married (dressed in deep mourning!) a long-devoted admirer, Dr John Bishop, a man as unlike Jim Nugent as it was possible to imagine. Conscientiously, Isabella took on the role of a respectable doctor's wife, but that many recognised its inherent unsuitability for her is suggested by a malicious story current at the time: Mrs Bishop, it was said, had intended to travel to New Guinea next, but gave up the idea because it wasn't the sort of place you could take a man to!

However, her kindly, mild-mannered husband lived but five years and in 1889, three years after his death when she was nearing sixty and was disconcertingly free from all emotional and family ties, Isabella embarked alone upon a number of truly intrepid expeditions into little-charted territory. Mounted on Arab horses, yaks, mountain ponies, she travelled in western Tibet and Ladakh, across the deserts of Persia and Kurdistan, into the isolated mountains of the Korean peninsula and, by junk and carry-chair, about three thousand miles through the remotest Chinese provinces. She left the Far East finally and with great reluctance in 1898, but even then she couldn't settle down in England. In her seventieth year she went on a last madcap fling to Morocco to visit the Berber Arabs in the Atlas Mountains, perched atop a huge black stallion which she mounted by climbing a ladder. In spite of all the privations and risks of her action-packed life, she died peacefully in bed in Edinburgh in 1904.

None of the later works, which describe the many journeys Isabella made after Henrietta's death, have the sparkle, the spontaneous, warm human understanding of her early books, of which *A Lady's Life in the Rocky Mountains* is the prime example. She had no one special to write her travel-letters to and for any more, and, from then on, she wrote, "The enjoyment though not the *interest* of travel has died out." Nor was she ever again remotely tempted by a man of Jim Nugent's ilk. Yet, the very fact that a woman of her age, background and education was once so tempted suggests the very disparate strains in her own personality.

Throughout her life, in the same small, squarish frame, there dwelt, on the one hand, the frail, decorous Victorian gentlewoman and, as she wrote to Henrietta from the Rockies, the indefatigable traveller with "an unconstrained manner and an up-to-anything, free-legged air"; the doctor's wife, firm upholder of the moral and social standards of her time, and the keen observer who described objectively (or with only occasional censure) the most outlandish customs, the most peculiar notions held by people on the opposite side of the world. Probably the most painful of Isabella's internal conflicts was between the conscientious Christian well schooled in the paths of duty, unselfishness and righteousness, and the "adventuress" – amoral, self-centred, unshockable, with a great lust for freedom and pleasure of all kinds who climbed the highest peaks in sight and warmed to the glint in Jim Nugent's eye.

Nor was Isabella ever able to reconcile these differing strains which, though they cost her much personal stress, undoubtedly goaded her into accomplishing as much as she did. It was sometimes said of her that she should have been a man – as it was said of many Victorian women of similar capacity

LETTER I.

LAKE TAHOE, *September 2.*

I HAVE found a dream of beauty at which one might
look all one's life and sigh. Not lovable, like the
Sandwich Islands, but beautiful in its own way!
A strictly North American beauty—snow-splotched
mountains, huge pines, red-woods, sugar pines, silver
spruce; a crystalline atmosphere, waves of the richest
colour; and a pine-hung lake which mirrors all beauty
on its surface. Lake Tahoe is before me, a sheet of
water twenty-two miles long by ten broad, and in
some places 1700 feet deep. It lies at a height of 6000
feet, and the snow-crowned summits which wall it in
are from 8000 to 11,000 feet in altitude. The air is
keen and elastic. There is no sound but the distant
and slightly musical ring of the lumberer's axe.

It is a weariness to go back, even in thought, to
the clang of San Francisco, which I left in its cold
morning fog early yesterday, driving to the Oakland

ferry through streets with side-walks heaped with thousands of cantaloupe and water-melons, tomatoes, cucumbers, squashes, pears, grapes, peaches, apricots, —all of startling size as compared with any I ever saw before. Other streets were piled with sacks of flour, left out all night, owing to the security from rain at this season. I pass hastily over the early part of the journey, the crossing the bay in a fog as chill as November, the number of "lunch baskets," which gave the car the look of conveying a great picnic party, the last view of the Pacific, on which I had looked for nearly a year, the fierce sunshine and brilliant sky inland, the look of long *rainlessness*, which one may not call drought, the valleys with sides crimson with the poison oak, the dusty vine-yards, with great purple clusters thick among the leaves, and between the vines great dusty melons lying on the dusty earth. From off the boundless harvest-fields the grain was carried in June, and it is now stacked in sacks along the track, awaiting freightage. California is a "land flowing with milk and honey." The barns are bursting with fulness. In the dusty orchards the apple and pear branches are supported, that they may not break down under the weight of fruit; melons, tomatoes, and squashes of gigantic size lie almost unheeded on the ground; fat cattle, gorged almost to repletion, shade them-selves under the oaks; superb "red" horses shine, not with grooming, but with condition; and thriving farms everywhere show on what a solid basis the prosperity of the "Golden State" is founded. Very uninviting, however rich, was the blazing Sacramento Valley, and very repulsive the city of Sacramento, which, at a distance of 125 miles from the Pacific, has an elevation of only thirty feet. The mercury stood at 103° in the shade, and the fine white dust was stifling.

In the late afternoon we began the ascent of the Sierras, whose saw-like points had been in sight for many miles. The dusty fertility was all left behind, the country became rocky and gravelly, and deeply scored by streams bearing the muddy wash of the mountain gold-mines down to the muddier Sacramento. There were long broken ridges and deep ravines, the ridges becoming longer, the ravines deeper, the pines thicker and larger, as we ascended into a cool atmosphere of exquisite purity, and before six P.M. the last traces of cultivation and the last hardwood trees were left behind.

At Colfax, a station at a height of 2400 feet, I got out and walked the length of the train. First came two great gaudy engines, the Grizzly Bear and the White Fox, with their respective tenders loaded with logs of wood, the engines with great, solitary, reflecting lamps in front above the cow-guards, a quantity of polished brass-work, comfortable glass houses, and well-stuffed seats for the engine-drivers. The engines and tenders were succeeded by a baggage-car, a mail-car, and Wells, Fargo, and Co.'s express-car, the latter loaded with bullion and valuable parcels, and in charge of two " express agents." Each of these cars is forty-five feet long. Then came two cars loaded with peaches and grapes; then two " silver palace" cars, each sixty feet long; then a smoking-car, at that time occupied mainly by Chinamen; and then five ordinary passenger-cars, with platforms like all the others, making altogether a train about 700 feet in length. The platforms of the four front cars were clustered over with Digger Indians, with their squaws, children, and gear. They are perfect savages, without any aptitude for even aboriginal civilisation, and are altogether the most degraded of the ill-fated tribes which are dying out before the white races. They were all very diminutive, five feet one inch being, I should think, about the average height, with flat noses, wide mouths, and black hair, cut straight above the eyes and hanging lank and long at the back and sides. The squaws wore their hair thickly plastered with pitch, and a broad band of the same across their noses and cheeks. They carried their infants on their backs, strapped to boards. The clothing of both sexes was a ragged, dirty combination of coarse woollen cloth and hide, the moccasins being unornamented. They were all hideous and filthy, and swarming with vermin. The men carried short bows and arrows, one of them, who appeared to be the chief, having a lynx's skin for a quiver. A few had fishing-tackle, but the bystanders said that they lived almost entirely upon grasshoppers. They were a most impressive incongruity in the midst of the tokens of an omnipotent civilisation.

The light of the sinking sun from that time glorified the Sierras, and as the dew fell, aromatic odours made the still air sweet. On a single track, sometimes carried on a narrow ledge excavated from the mountain side by men lowered from the top in baskets, overhanging ravines from 2000 to 3000 feet deep, the monster train *snaked* its way upwards, stopping sometimes in front of a few frame houses, at others where nothing was to be seen but a log cabin with a few Chinamen hanging about it, but where trails on the sides of the ravines pointed to a gold country above and below. So sharp and frequent are the curves on some parts of the ascent, that on looking out of the window one could seldom see more than a part of the train at once. At Cape Horn, where the track curves round the ledge of a precipice 2500 feet in depth, it is correct to be frightened, and a fashion of holding the breath and shutting the eyes prevails, but my fears were reserved for the crossing of a trestle-bridge over a very deep chasm, which is itself approached by a sharp curve. This bridge appeared to be overlapped by the cars so as to produce the effect of looking down directly into a wild gulch, with a torrent raging along it at an immense depth below.

Shivering in the keen, frosty air near the summit-pass of the Sierras, we entered the "snow-sheds," wooden galleries, which for about fifty miles shut out all the splendid views of the region, as given in dioramas, not even allowing a glimpse of "the Gem of the Sierras," the lovely Donner Lake. One of these sheds is twenty-seven miles long. In a few hours the mercury had fallen from 103° to 29°, and we had ascended 6987 feet in 105 miles! After passing through the sheds, we had several grand views of a pine-forest on fire before reaching Truckee at 11 P.M., having travelled 258 miles. Truckee, the centre of the "lumbering region" of the Sierras, is usually spoken of as "a rough mountain town," and Mr. W. had told me that all the roughs of the district congregated there, that there were nightly pistol affrays in bar-rooms, etc., but as he admitted that a lady was sure of respect, and Mr. G. strongly advised me to stay and see the lakes, I got out, much dazed, and very stupid with sleep, envying the people in the sleeping-car, who were already unconscious on their luxurious couches. The cars drew up in a street— if street that could be called which was only a wide, cleared space, intersected by rails, with here and there a stump, and great piles of sawn logs bulking big in the moonlight, and a number of irregular clap-board, steep-roofed houses, many of them with open fronts, glaring with light and crowded with men. We had pulled up at the door of a rough Western hotel, with a partially open front, being a bar-room crowded with men drinking and smoking, and the space between it and the cars was a moving mass of loafers and passengers. On the tracks, engines, tolling heavy bells, were mightily moving, the glare from their cyclopean eyes dulling the light of a forest which was burning fitfully on a mountain side; and on open spaces great fires of pine-logs were burning cheerily, with groups of men round them. A band was playing noisily, and the unholy sound of tom-toms was not far off. Mountains—the sierras of many a fireside dream— seemed to wall in the town, and great pines stood out, sharp and clear cut, against a sky in which a moon and stars were shining frostily.

It was a sharp frost at that great height, and when an "irrepressible nigger," who seemed to represent the hotel establishment, deposited me and my carpet-bag in a room which answered for "the parlour," I was glad to find some remains of pine knots still alight in the stove. A man came in and said that when the cars were gone he would try to get me a room, but they were so full that it would be a very poor one. The crowd was solely masculine. It was then 11.30 P.M., and I had not had a meal since 6

A.M.; but when I asked hopefully for a hot supper, with tea, I was told that no supper could be got at that hour; but in half an hour the same man returned with a small cup of cold, weak tea, and a small slice of bread, which looked as if it had been much handled.

I asked the negro factotum about the hire of horses, and presently a man came in from the bar who, he said, could supply my needs. This man, the very type of a western pioneer, bowed, threw himself into a rocking-chair, drew a spittoon beside him, cut a fresh quid of tobacco, began to chew energetically, and put his feet, cased in miry high boots, into which his trousers were tucked, on the top of the stove. He said he had horses which would both "lope" and trot, that some ladies preferred the Mexican saddle, that I could ride alone in perfect safety; and after a route had been devised, I hired a horse for two days. This man wore a pioneer's badge as one of the earliest settlers of California, but he had moved on as one place after another had become too civilised for him, "but nothing," he added, "was likely to change much in Truckee." I was afterwards told that the usual regular hours of sleep are not observed there. The accommodation is too limited for the population of 2000,[1] which is masculine mainly, and is liable to frequent temporary additions, and beds are occupied continuously, though by different

[1] Nelson's *Guide to the Central Pacific Railroad.*

occupants, throughout the greater part of the twenty-four hours. Consequently I found the bed and room allotted to me quite tumbled-looking. Men's coats and sticks were hanging up, miry boots were littered about, and a rifle was in one corner. There was no window to the outer air, but I slept soundly, being only once awoke by an increase of the same din in which I had fallen asleep, varied by three pistol-shots fired in rapid succession.

This morning Truckee wore a totally different aspect. The crowds of the night before had disappeared. There were heaps of ashes where the fires had been. A sleepy German waiter seemed the only person about the premises, the open drinking-saloons were nearly empty, and only a few sleepy-looking loafers hung about in what is called the street. It might have been Sunday; but they say that it brings a great accession of throng and jollity. Public worship has died out at present; work is discontinued on Sunday, but the day is given up to pleasure. Putting a minimum of indispensables into a bag, and slipping on my Hawaiian riding-dress over a silk skirt, and a dust-cloak over all, I stealthily crossed the *plaza* to the livery-stable, the largest building in Truckee, where twelve fine horses were stabled in stalls on each side of a broad drive. My friend of the evening before showed me his " rig," three velvet-covered side-saddles almost without horns. Some

ladies, he said, used the horn of the Mexican saddle,
but none "in this part" rode cavalier fashion. I felt
abashed. I could not ride any distance in the conventional mode, and was just going to give up this
splendid "ravage," when the man said, "Ride your
own fashion; here, at Truckee, if anywhere in the
world, people can do as they like." Blissful Truckee!
In no time a large grey horse was "rigged out" in a
handsome silver-bossed Mexican saddle, with ornamental leather tassels hanging from the stirrup-
guards, and a housing of black bear's-skin.   I
strapped my silk skirt on the saddle, deposited my
cloak in the corn-bin, and was safely on the horse's
back before his owner had time to devise any way
of mounting me. Neither he nor any of the loafers
who had assembled showed the slightest sign of
astonishment, but all were as respectful as possible.

Once on horseback my embarrassment disappeared, and I rode through Truckee, whose irregular,
steep-roofed houses and shanties, set down in a
clearing, and surrounded closely by mountain and
forest, looked like a temporary encampment, passed
under the Pacific Railroad, and then for twelve miles
followed the windings of the Truckee river, a clear,
rushing, mountain stream, in which immense pine
logs had gone aground not to be floated off till the
next freshet, a loud-tongued, rollicking stream of ice-
cold water, on whose banks no ferns or trailers hang,

and which leaves no greenness along its turbulent
progress. All was bright with that brilliancy of sky
and atmosphere, that blaze of sunshine and universal
glitter, which I never saw till I came to California,
combined with an elasticity in the air which removes
all lassitude, and gives one spirit enough for anything. On either side of the Truckee great sierras
rose like walls, castellated, embattled, rifted, skirted
and crowned with pines of enormous size, the walls
now and then breaking apart to show some snow-
slashed peak rising into a heaven of intense, un-
clouded, sunny blue. At this altitude of 6000 feet
one must learn to be content with varieties of *coniferæ*, for, except for aspens, which spring up in some
places where the pines have been cleared away, and
for cotton-woods, which at a lower level fringe the
streams, there is nothing but the bear cherry, the
raspberry, the gooseberry, the wild grape, and the
wild currant. None of these grew near the Truckee,
but I feasted my eyes on pines [1] which, though not so
large as the Wellingtonia of the Yosemite, are really
gigantic, attaining a height of 250 feet, their huge
stems, the warm red of cedar wood, rising straight
and branchless for a third of their height, their
diameter from seven to fifteen feet, their shape
that of a larch, but with the needles long and dark,
and cones a foot long. Pines cleft the sky; they

[1] *Pinus Lambertiana.*

were massed wherever level ground occurred; they
stood over the Truckee at right angles, or lay across
it in prostrate grandeur. Their stumps and carcasses
were everywhere; and smooth "shoots" on the
sierras marked where they were shot down as "felled
timber," to be floated off by the river. To them this
wild region owes its scattered population, and the
sharp ring of the lumberer's axe mingles with the
cries of wild beasts and the roar of mountain torrents.

The track is a soft, natural, waggon road, very
pleasant to ride on. The horse was much too big for
me, and had plans of his own; but now and then,
where the ground admitted of it, I tried his heavy
"lope" with much amusement. I met nobody, and
passed nothing on the road but a freight waggon,
drawn by twenty-two oxen, guided by three fine-
looking young men, who had some difficulty in
making room for me to pass their awkward convoy.
After I had ridden about ten miles the road went up
a steep hill in the forest, turned abruptly, and through
the blue gloom of the great pines which rose from
the ravine in which the river was then hid, came
glimpses of two mountains, about 11,000 feet in
height, whose bald grey summits were crowned with
pure snow. It was one of those glorious surprises in
scenery which make one feel as if one must bow
down and worship. The forest was thick, and had
an undergrowth of dwarf spruce and brambles, but

as the horse had become fidgety and "scary" on the track, I turned off in the idea of taking a short cut, and was sitting carelessly, shortening my stirrup, when a great, dark, hairy beast rose, crashing and snorting, out of the tangle just in front of me. I had only a glimpse of him, and thought that my imagination had magnified a wild boar, but it was a bear. The horse snorted and plunged violently, as if he would go down to the river, and then turned, still plunging, up a steep bank, when, finding that I must come off, I threw myself off on the right side, where the ground rose considerably, so that I had not far to fall. I got up covered with dust, but neither shaken nor bruised. It was truly grotesque and humiliating. The bear ran in one direction, and the horse in another. I hurried after the latter, and twice he stopped till I was close to him, then turned round and cantered away. After walking about a mile in deep dust, I picked up first the saddle-blanket and next my bag, and soon came upon the horse, standing facing me, and shaking all over. I thought I should catch him then, but when I went up to him he turned round, threw up his heels several times, rushed off the track, galloped in circles, bucking, kicking, and plunging for some time, and then throwing up his heels as an act of final defiance, went off at full speed in the direction of Truckee, with the saddle over his shoulders and the great

"living light," exquisite chipmonks ran across the track, but only a dusty blue lupin here and there reminded me of earth's fairer children.   Then the river became broad and still, and mirrored in its transparent depths regal pines, straight as an arrow, with rich yellow and green lichen clinging to their stems, and firs and balsam-pines filling up the spaces between them, the gorge opened, and this mountain-girdled lake lay before me, with its margin broken up into bays and promontories, most picturesquely clothed by huge sugar-pines.   It lay dimpling and scintillating beneath the noonday sun, as entirely unspoilt as fifteen years ago, when its pure loveliness was known only to trappers and Indians.   One man lives on it the whole year round ; otherwise early October strips its shores of their few inhabitants, and thereafter, for seven months, it is rarely accessible except on snow-shoes.   It never freezes.   In the dense forests which bound it, and drape two-thirds of its gaunt sierras, are hordes of grizzlies, brown bears, wolves, elk, deer, chipmonks, martens, minks, skunks, foxes, squirrels, and snakes.   On its margin I found an irregular wooden inn, with a lumber-waggon at the door, on which was the carcass of a large grizzly bear, shot behind the house this morning.   I had intended to ride ten miles farther, but, finding that the trail in some places was a "blind" one, and being bewitched by the beauty and serenity

LETTER II.

A Lady's "Get-up"—Grizzly Bears—The "Gem of the Sierras"
—A Tragic Tale—A Carnival of Colour.

CHEYENNE, WYOMING, *September* 7.

As night came on the cold intensified, and the stove
in the parlour attracted every one.   A San Francisco
lady, much "got up" in paint, emerald green velvet,
Brussels lace, and diamonds, rattled continuously
for the amusement of the company, giving descriptions of persons and scenes in a racy Western twang,
without the slightest scruple as to what she said.
In a few years Tahoe will be inundated in summer
with similar vulgarity, owing to its easiness of access.
I sustained the reputation which our countrywomen
bear in America by looking a "perfect guy;" and
feeling that I was a salient point for the speaker's
next sally, I was relieved when the landlady, a
ladylike Englishwoman, asked me to join herself
and her family in the bar-room, where we had much
talk about the neighbourhood and its wild beasts,
especially bears.   The forest is full of them, but
they seem never to attack people unless when

wounded, or much aggravated by dogs, or a she-bear thinks you are going to molest her young.

I dreamt of bears so vividly that I woke with a furry death-hug at my throat, but feeling quite refreshed. When I mounted my horse after break-fast the sun was high and the air so keen and intoxi-cating that, giving the animal his head, I galloped up and down hill, feeling completely tireless. Truly, that air is the elixir of life. I had a glorious ride back to Truckee. The road was not as solitary as the day before. In a deep part of the forest the horse snorted and reared, and I saw a cinnamon-coloured bear with two cubs cross the track ahead of me. I tried to keep the horse quiet that the mother might acquit me of any designs upon her lolloping children, but I was glad when the ungainly, long-haired party crossed the river. Then I met a team, the driver of which stopped and said he was glad that I had not gone to Cornelian Bay, it was such a bad trail, and hoped I had enjoyed Tahoe. The driver of another team stopped and asked if I had seen any bears. Then a man heavily armed, a hunter probably, asked me if I were the English tourist who had "happened on" a "grizzlie" yesterday. Then I saw a lumberer taking his dinner on a rock in the river, who "touched his hat" and brought me a draught of ice-cold water, which I could hardly drink owing to the fractiousness of the horse, and gathered me some mountain pinks, which I admired. I mention these little incidents to indicate the habit of respectful courtesy to women which prevails in that region. These men might have been excused for speaking in a somewhat free-and-easy tone to a lady riding alone, and in an unwonted fashion. Womanly dignity and manly respect for women are the salt of society in this wild West.

My horse was so excitable that I avoided the centre of Truckee, and skulked through a collection of Chinamen's shanties to the stable, where a prodigious roan horse, standing seventeen hands high, was produced for my ride to the Donner Lake. I asked the owner, who was as interested in my enjoying myself as a West Highlander might have been, if there were not ruffians about who might make an evening ride dangerous. A story was current of a man having ridden through Truckee two evenings before with a chopped-up human body in a sack behind the saddle, and hosts of stories of ruffianism are located there, rightly or wrongly. This man said, "There's a bad breed of ruffians, but the ugliest among them all won't touch you. There's nothing Western folk admire so much as pluck in a woman." I had to get on a barrel before I could reach the stirrup, and when I was mounted my feet only came half-way down the horse's sides. I felt like a fly on him. The road at first lay through a valley without a river, but some swampishness nourished some rank swamp-grass, the first *green* grass I have seen in America; and the pines, with their red stems, looked beautiful rising out of it. I hurried along, and came upon the Donner Lake quite suddenly, to be completely smitten by its beauty. It is only about three miles long by one and a half broad, and lies hidden away among mountains, with no dwellings on its shores but some deserted lumberers' cabins.[1] Its loneliness pleased me well. I did not see man, beast, or bird from the time I left Truckee till I returned. The mountains, which rise abruptly from the margin, are covered with dense pine-forests, through which, here and there, strange forms of bare grey rock, castellated, or needle-like, protrude themselves. On the opposite side, at a height of about 6000 feet, a grey, ascending line, from which rumbling, incoherent sounds occasionally proceeded, is seen through the pines. This is one of the snow-sheds of the Pacific Railroad, which shuts out from travellers all that I was seeing. The lake is called after Mr. Donner, who, with his family, arrived at the Truckee river in the fall of the year, in company with a party of emigrants bound for California. Being encumbered with many cattle, he let the company pass on, and, with his own party of sixteen souls, which included his wife and four children, encamped by the lake.

[1] Visitors can now be accommodated at a tolerable mountain hotel.

In the morning they found themselves surrounded by an expanse of snow, and after some consultation it was agreed that the whole party except Mr. Donner, who was unwell, his wife, and a German friend, should take the horses and attempt to cross the mountain, which, after much peril, they succeeded in doing; but, as the storm continued for several weeks, it was impossible for any rescue party to succour the three who had been left behind. In the early spring, when the snow was hard enough for travelling, a party started in quest, expecting to find the snow-bound alive and well, as they had cattle enough for their support, and, after weeks of toil and exposure, they scaled the Sierras and reached the Donner Lake. On arriving at the camp they opened the rude door, and there, sitting before the fire, they found the German, holding a roasted human arm and hand, which he was greedily eating. The rescue party overpowered him, and with difficulty tore the arm from him. A short search discovered the body of the lady, minus the arm, frozen in the snow, round, plump, and fair, showing that she was in perfect health when she met her fate. The rescuers returned to California, taking the German with them, whose story was that Mr. Donner died in the fall, and that the cattle escaped, leaving them but little food, and that when this was exhausted Mrs. Donner died. The story never gained any credence, and the

truth oozed out that the German had murdered the
husband, then brutally murdered the wife, and had
seized upon Donner's money. There were, however,
no witnesses, and the murderer escaped with the
enforced surrender of the money to the Donner
orphans.

This tragic story filled my mind as I rode towards
the head of the lake, which became every moment
grander and more unutterably lovely. The sun was
setting fast, and against his golden light green promontories, wooded with stately pines, stood out one
beyond another in a medium of dark rich blue, while
grey bleached summits, peaked, turreted, and snow-
slashed, were piled above them, gleaming with amber
light. Darker grew the blue gloom, the dew fell
heavily, aromatic odours floated on the air, and still
the lofty peaks glowed with living light, till in one
second it died off from them, leaving them with the
ashy paleness of a dead face. It was dark and cold
under the mountain shadows, the frosty chill of the
high altitude wrapped me round, the solitude was
overwhelming, and I reluctantly turned my horse's
head towards Truckee, often looking back to the
ashy summits in their unearthly fascination. East-
wards the look of the scenery was changing every
moment, while the lake for long remained "one
burnished sheet of living gold," and Truckee lay
utterly out of sight in a hollow filled with lake and

cobalt. Before long a carnival of colour began which
I can only describe as delirious, intoxicating, a hardly
bearable joy, a tender anguish, an indescribable
yearning, an unearthly music, rich in love and
worship. It lasted considerably more than an hour,
and though the road was growing very dark, and
the train which was to take me thence was fast
climbing the Sierras, I could not ride faster than a
walk.

The eastward mountains, which had been grey,
blushed pale pink, the pink deepened into rose, and
the rose into crimson, and then all solidityethereal-
ised away and became clear and pure as an amethyst,
while all the waving ranges and the broken pine-
clothed ridges below etherealised too, but into a dark
rich blue, and a strange effect of atmosphere blended
the whole into one perfect picture. It changed,
deepened, reddened, melted, growing more and more
wonderful, while under the pines it was night, till,
having displayed itself for an hour, the jewelled
peaks suddenly became like those of the sierras, wan
as the face of death. Far later the cold golden light
lingered in the west, with pines in relief against its
purity, and where the rose light had glowed in the
east, a huge moon upheaved itself, and the red flicker
of forest fires luridly streaked the mountain sides
near and far off. I realised that night had come
with its *eeriness*, and putting my great horse into a

LETTER III.

A Temple of Morpheus—Utah—A "God-forgotten" Town—A distressed Couple — Dog Villages — A Temperance Colony—A Colorado Inn—The Bug pest—Fort Collins.

CHEYENNE, WYOMING, *September 8.*

PRECISELY at 11 P.M. the huge Pacific train, with its heavy bell tolling, thundered up to the door of the Truckee House, and on presenting my ticket at the double door of a "Silver Palace" car, the slippered steward, whispering low, conducted me to my berth— a luxurious bed three and a half feet wide, with a hair mattress on springs, fine linen sheets, and costly California blankets.   The twenty-four inmates of the car were all invisible, asleep behind rich curtains.   It was a true Temple of Morpheus.   Profound sleep was the object to which everything was dedicated.   Four silver lamps hanging from the roof, and burning low, gave a dreamy light.   On each side of the centre passage, rich rep curtains, green and crimson, striped with gold, hung from silver bars running near the roof, and trailed on the soft Axminster carpet.   The temperature was carefully kept at 70°.   It was 29° outside.   Silence and freedom from jolting were secured by double doors and windows, costly and ingenious arrangements of springs and cushions, and a speed limited to eighteen miles an hour.

As I lay down, the gallop under the dark pines, the frosty moon, the forest fires, the flaring lights and roaring din of Truckee faded as dreams fade, and eight hours later a pure, pink dawn divulged a level blasted region, with grey sage brush growing out of a soil encrusted with alkali, and bounded on either side by low glaring ridges. All through that day we travelled under a cloudless sky over solitary glaring plains, and stopped twice at solitary, glaring frame houses, where coarse, greasy meals, infested by lazy flies, were provided at a dollar per head. By evening we were running across the continent on a bee line, and I sat for an hour on the rear platform of the rear car to enjoy the wonderful beauty of the sunset and the atmosphere. Far as one could see in the crystalline air there was nothing but desert. The jagged Humboldt ranges flaming in the sunset, with snow in their clefts, though forty-five miles off, looked within an easy canter. The bright metal track, purpling like all else in the cool distance, was all that linked one with eastern or western civilisation.

The next morning, when the steward unceremoniously turned us out of our berths soon after sunrise, we were running down upon the Great Salt Lake, bounded by the white Wahsatch ranges.

Along its shores, by means of irrigation, Mormon industry has compelled the ground to yield fine crops of hay and barley; and we passed several cabins, from which, even at that early hour, Mormons, each with two or three wives, were going forth to their day's work. The women were ugly, and their shapeless blue dresses hideous. At the Mormon town of Ogden we changed cars, and again traversed dusty plains, white and glaring, varied by muddy streams and rough, arid valleys, now and then narrowing into canyons. By common consent the windows were kept closed to exclude the fine white alkaline dust, which is very irritating to the nostrils. The journey became more and more wearisome as we ascended rapidly over immense plains and wastes of gravel destitute of mountain boundaries, and with only here and there a "knob" or "butte"[1] to break the monotony. The wheel marks of the trail to Utah often ran parallel with the track, and bones of oxen were bleaching in the sun, the remains of those "whose carcasses fell in the wilderness" on the long and drouthy journey. The daybreak of to-day (Sunday) found us shivering at Fort Laramie, a frontier post dismally situated at a height of 7000 feet. Another 1000 feet over gravelly levels brought us to Sherman, the highest

[1] The mountains which bound the "Valley of the Babbling Waters," Utah, afford striking examples of these "knobs" or "buttes."

level reached by this railroad. From this point eastward the streams fall into the Atlantic. The ascent
of these apparently level plateaus is called "crossing
the Rocky Mountains," but I have seen nothing of
the range, except two peaks like teeth lying low on
the distant horizon. It became mercilessly cold;
some people thought it snowed, but I only saw rolling billows of fog. Lads passed through the cars the
whole morning, selling newspapers, novels, cacti,
lollypops, pop corn, pea nuts, and ivory ornaments,
so that, having lost all reckoning of the days, I never
knew that it was Sunday till the cars pulled up at
the door of the hotel in this detestable place.

The surrounding plains are endless and verdure-
less. The scanty grasses were long ago turned into
sun-cured hay by the fierce summer heats. There is
neither tree nor bush, the sky is grey, the earth buff,
the air *blae* and windy, and clouds of coarse granitic
dust sweep across the prairie and smother the settlement. Cheyenne is described as "a God-forsaken,
God-forgotten place." That it forgets God is written
on its face. It owes its existence to the railroad,
and has diminished in population, but is a depôt for
a large amount of the necessaries of life which are
distributed through the scantily settled districts within
distances of 300 miles by "freight waggons," each
drawn by four or six horses or mules, or double that
number of oxen. At times over 100 waggons, with

double that number of teamsters, are in Cheyenne at once. A short time ago it was a perfect pandemonium, mainly inhabited by rowdies and desperadoes, the scum of advancing civilisation; and murders, stabbings, shootings, and pistol affrays were at times events of almost hourly occurrence in its drinking dens. But in the West, when things reach their worst, a sharp and sure remedy is provided. Those settlers who find the state of matters intolerable, organise themselves into a Vigilance Committee. "Judge Lynch," with a few feet of rope, appears on the scene, the majority crystallises round the supporters of order, warnings are issued to obnoxious people, simply bearing a scrawl of a tree with a man dangling from it, with such words as "Clear out of this by 6 A.M., or ——." A number of the worst desperadoes are tried by a yet more summary process than a drumhead court-martial, "strung up," and buried ignominiously. I have been told that 120 ruffians were disposed of in this way here in a single fortnight. Cheyenne is now as safe as Hilo, and the interval between the most desperate lawlessness and the time when United States law, with its corruption and feebleness, comes upon the scene is one of comparative security and good order. Piety is not the *forte* of Cheyenne. The roads resound with atrocious profanity, and the rowdyism of the saloons and barrooms is repressed, not extirpated.

The population, once 6000, is now about 4000. It is an ill-arranged set of frame houses and shanties;[1] and rubbish heaps, and offal of deer and antelope, produce the foulest smells I have smelt for a long time. Some of the houses are painted a blinding white; others are unpainted; there is not a bush, or garden, or green thing; it just straggles out promiscuously on the boundless brown plains, on the extreme verge of which three toothy peaks are seen. It is utterly slovenly-looking and unornamental, abounds in slouching bar-room-looking characters, and looks a place of low, mean lives. Below the hotel windows freight cars are being perpetually shunted, but beyond the railroad tracks are nothing but the brown plains, with their lonely sights—now a solitary horseman at a travelling amble, then a party of Indians in paint and feathers, but civilised up to the point of carrying firearms, mounted on sorry ponies, the bundled-up squaws riding astride on the baggage-ponies; then a drove of ridgy-spined, long-horned cattle, which have been several months eating their way from Texas, with their escort of four or five much-spurred horsemen, in peaked hats, blue-hooded coats, and high boots, heavily armed with revolvers and repeating rifles, and riding small wiry horses. A solitary wag-

[1] The discovery of gold in the Black Hills has lately given it a great impetus, and as it is the chief point of departure for the diggings, it is increasing in population and importance.—July 1879.

gon, with a white tilt, drawn by eight oxen, is probably bearing an emigrant and his fortunes to Colorado. On one of the dreary spaces of the settlement
six white-tilted waggons, each with twelve oxen, are
standing on their way to a distant part. Everything
suggests a beyond.

September 9.

I have found at the post-office here a circular
letter of recommendation from ex-Governor Hunt,
procured by Miss Kingsley's kindness, and another equally valuable one of " authentication " and
recommendation from Mr. Bowles, of the *Springfield
Republican,* whose name is a household word in all
the West. Armed with these, I shall plunge boldly
into Colorado. I am suffering from giddiness and
nausea produced by the bad smells. A " help " here
says that there have been fifty-six deaths from cholera
during the last twenty days. Is common humanity
lacking, I wonder, in this region of hard greed? Can
it not be bought by dollars here, like every other
commodity, votes included? Last night I made the
acquaintance of a shadowy gentleman from Wiscon-
sin, far gone in consumption, with a spirited wife and
young baby. He had been ordered to the Plains as
a last resource, but was much worse. Early this
morning he crawled to my door, scarcely able to
speak from debility and bleeding from the lungs,
begging me to go to his wife, who, the doctor said,

was ill of cholera. The child had been ill all night, and not for love or money could he get any one to do anything for them, not even to go for the medicine. The lady was blue, and in great pain from cramp, and the poor unweaned infant was roaring for the nourishment which had failed. I vainly tried to get hot water and mustard for a poultice, and though I offered a negro a dollar to go for the medicine, he looked at it superciliously, hummed a tune, and said he must wait for the Pacific train, which was not due for an hour. Equally in vain I hunted through Cheyenne for a feeding-bottle. Not a maternal heart softened to the helpless mother and starving child, and my last resource was to dip a piece of sponge in some milk and water, and try to pacify the creature. I applied Rigollot's leaves, went for the medicine, saw the popular host—a bachelor—who mentioned a girl who, after much difficulty, consented to take charge of the baby for two dollars a day and attend to the mother, and having remained till she began to amend, I took the cars for Greeley, a settlement on the Plains, which I had been recommended to make my starting-point for the mountains.

FORT COLLINS, *September 10.*

It gave me a strange sensation to embark upon the Plains. Plains, plains everywhere, plains generally level, but elsewhere rolling in long undulations, like the waves of a sea which had fallen asleep. They are covered thinly with buff grass, the withered stalks of flowers, Spanish bayonet, and a small beehive-shaped cactus. One could gallop all over them.

They are peopled with large villages of what are called prairie dogs, because they utter a short, sharp bark, but the dogs are, in reality, marmots. We passed numbers of these villages, which are composed of raised circular orifices, about eighteen inches in diameter, with sloping passages leading downwards for five or six feet. Hundreds of these burrows are placed together. On nearly every rim a small furry reddish-buff beast sat on his hind legs, looking, so far as head went, much like a young seal. These creatures were acting as sentinels, and sunning themselves. As we passed, each gave a warning yelp, shook its tail, and, with a ludicrous flourish of its hind legs, dived into its hole. The appearance of hundreds of these creatures, each eighteen inches long, sitting like dogs begging, with their paws down and all turned sunwards, is most grotesque. The Wish-ton-Wish has few enemies, and is a most prolific animal. From its enormous increase, and the energy and extent of its burrowing operations, one can fancy that in the course of years the prairies will be seriously injured, as it honeycombs the ground, and renders it unsafe for horses. The burrows seem usually to be shared by owls, and many of the people insist that a rattlesnake is also an inmate, but I hope,

for the sake of the harmless, cheery little prairie dog,
that this unwelcome fellowship is a myth.

After running on a down grade for some time,
five distinct ranges of mountains, one above another,
a lurid blue against a lurid sky, upheaved themselves
above the prairie sea. An American railway car,
hot, stuffy, and full of chewing, spitting Yankees,
was not an ideal way of approaching this range
which had early impressed itself upon my imagination.   Still, it was truly grand, although it was sixty
miles off, and we were looking at it from a platform
5000 feet in height.   As I write I am only twenty-
five miles from them, and they are gradually gaining
possession of me.   I can look at and *feel* nothing
else.   At five in the afternoon frame houses and
green fields began to appear, the cars drew up, and
two of my fellow-passengers and I got out and carried
our own luggage through the deep dust to a small,
rough, Western tavern, where with difficulty we were
put up for the night.   This settlement is called the
Greeley Temperance Colony, and was founded lately
by an industrious class of emigrants from the East,
all total abstainers, and holding advanced political
opinions.   They bought and fenced 50,000 acres of
land, constructed an irrigating canal, which distri-
butes its waters on reasonable terms, have already a
population of 3000, and are the most prosperous and
rising colony in Colorado, being altogether free from

either laziness or crime. Their rich fields are artificially productive solely; and after seeing regions where Nature gives spontaneously, one is amazed that people should settle here to be dependent on irrigating canals, with the risk of having their crops destroyed by grasshoppers. A clause in the charter of the colony prohibits the introduction, sale, or consumption of intoxicating liquor, and I hear that the men of Greeley carry their crusade against drink even beyond their limits, and have lately sacked three houses opened for the sale of drink near their frontier, pouring the whisky upon the ground, so that people don't now like to run the risk of bringing liquor near Greeley, and the temperance influence is spreading over a very large area. As the men have no bar-rooms to sit in, I observed that Greeley was asleep at an hour when other places were beginning their revelries. Nature is niggardly, and living is coarse and rough, the merest necessaries of hardy life being all that can be thought of in this stage of existence.

My first experiences of Colorado travel have been rather severe. At Greeley I got a small upstairs room at first, but gave it up to a married couple with a child, and then had one downstairs no bigger than a cabin, with only a canvas partition. It was very hot, and every place was thick with black flies. The English landlady had just lost her " help," and was in a great fuss, so that I helped her to get supper ready.

for a long journey; and as my Vermont acquaintance offered me a seat in his waggon to Fort Collins, 25 miles nearer the Mountains, I threw a few things together and came here with him. We left Greeley at 10, and arrived here at 4.30, staying an hour for food on the way. I liked the first half of the drive; but the fierce, ungoverned, blazing heat of the sun on the whitish earth for the last half, was terrible even with my white umbrella, which I have not used since I left New Zealand; it was sickening. Then the eyes have never anything green to rest upon, except in the river bottoms, where there is green hay grass. We followed mostly the course of the River Cache-a-la-Poudre, which rises in the mountains, and after supplying Greeley with irrigation, falls into the Platte, which is an affluent of the Missouri. When once beyond the scattered houses and great ring fence of the vigorous Greeley colonists, we were on the boundless prairie. Now and then horsemen passed us, and we met three waggons with white tilts. Except where the prairie dogs have honeycombed the ground, you can drive almost anywhere, and the passage of a few waggons over the same track makes a road. We forded the river, whose course is marked the whole way by a fringe of small cotton woods and aspens, and travelled hour after hour with nothing to see except some dog towns, with their quaint little sentinels; but the view in front was glorious. The *vacheros*, heavily armed, and a light waggon accompanied them, full of extra rifles and ammunition, not unnecessary, for the Indians are raiding in all directions, maddened by the reckless and useless slaughter of the buffalo, which is their chief subsistence. On the plains are herds of wild horses, buffalo, deer, and antelope; and in the mountains, bears, wolves, deer, elk, mountain lions, bison, and mountain sheep. You see a rifle in every waggon, as people always hope to fall in with game.

By the time we reached Fort Collins I was sick and dizzy with the heat of the sun, and not disposed to be pleased with a most unpleasing place. It was a military post, but at present consists of a few frame houses put down recently on the bare and burning plain. The settlers have "great expectations," but of what? The mountains look hardly nearer than from Greeley; one only realises their vicinity by the loss of their higher peaks. This house is freer from bugs than the one at Greeley, but full of flies. These new settlements are altogether revolting, entirely utilitarian, given up to talk of dollars as well as to making them, with coarse speech, coarse food, coarse everything, nothing wherewith to satisfy the higher cravings if they exist, nothing on which the eye can rest with pleasure. The lower floor of this inn swarms with locusts in addition to thousands of black flies. The latter cover the ground and rise buzzing from it as you walk.   I. L. B.

LETTER IV.

A Plague of Flies—A melancholy Charioteer—The Foot Hills—A
Mountain Boarding-House—A dull Life—" Being Agreeable "—
Climate of Colorado—*Soroche* and Snakes.

CANYON, *September 12.*

I WAS actually so dull and tired that I deliberately
slept away the afternoon in order to forget the heat
and flies.   Thirty men in working clothes, silent and
sad-looking, came in to supper.   The beef was tough
and greasy, the butter had turned to oil, and beef and
butter were black with living, drowned, and half-
drowned flies.   The greasy table-cloth was black also
with flies, and I did not wonder that the guests looked
melancholy and quickly escaped. I failed to get a horse,
but was strongly recommended to come here and board
with a settler, who, they said, had a saw-mill and
took boarders.   The person who recommended it so
strongly gave me a note of introduction, and told me
that it was in a grand part of the mountains, where
many people had been camping out all the summer
for the benefit of their health.   The idea of a boarding-house, as I know them in America, was rather
formidable in the present state of my wardrobe, and

I decided on bringing my carpet-bag, as well as my pack, lest I should be rejected for my bad clothes. Early the next morning I left in a buggy drawn by light *broncos* and driven by a profoundly melancholy young man. He had never been to the canyon; there was no road. We met nobody, saw nothing except antelope in the distance, and he became more melancholy and lost his way, driving hither and thither for about twenty miles till we came upon an old trail which eventually brought us to a fertile " bottom," where hay and barley were being harvested, and five or six frame houses looked cheerful. I had been recommended to two of these, which professed to take in strangers, but one was full of reapers, and in the other a child was dead. So I took the buggy on, glad to leave the glaring, prosaic settlement behind. There was a most curious loneliness about the journey up to that time. Except for the huge barrier to the right, the boundless prairies were everywhere, and it was like being at sea without a compass. The wheels made neither sound nor indentation as we drove over the short, dry grass, and there was no cheerful clatter of horses' hoofs. The sky was cloudy and the air hot and still. In one place we passed the carcass of a mule, and a number of vultures soared up from it, to descend again immediately. Skeletons and bones of animals were often to be seen. A range of low, grassy hills, called the

Foot Hills, rose from the plain, featureless and monotonous, except where streams, fed by the snows of the higher regions, had cut their way through them. Confessedly bewildered, and more melancholy than ever, the driver turned up one of the widest of these entrances, and in another hour the Foot Hills lay between us and the prairie sea, and a higher and broken range, with pitch pines of average size, was revealed behind them. These Foot Hills, which swell up uninterestingly from the plains on their eastern side, on their western have the appearance of having broken off from the next range, and the break is abrupt, and takes the form of walls and terraces of rock of the most brilliant colour, weathered and stained by ores, and, even under the grey sky, dazzling to the eyes. The driver thought he had understood the directions given, but he was stupid, and once we lost some miles by arriving at a river too rough and deep to be forded, and again we were brought up by an impassable canyon. He grew frightened about his horses, and said no money would ever tempt him into the mountains again; but average intelligence would have made it all easy.

The solitude was becoming sombre, when, after driving for nine hours, and travelling at the least forty-five miles, without any sign of fatigue on the part of the *broncos*, we came to a stream, by the side of which we drove along a definite track, till we came to a sort of tripartite valley, with a majestic crooked canyon 2000 feet deep opening upon it. A rushing stream roared through it, and the Rocky Mountains, with pines scattered over them, came down upon it. A little farther, and the canyon became utterly inaccessible. This was exciting; here was an inner world. A rough and shaky bridge, made of the outsides of pines laid upon some unsecured logs, crossed the river. The *broncos* stopped and smelt it, not liking it, but some encouraging speech induced them to go over. On the other side was a log cabin, partially ruinous, and the very rudest I ever saw, its roof of plastered mud being broken into large holes. It stood close to the water among some cotton-wood trees. A little higher there was a very primitive saw-mill, also out of repair, with some logs lying about. An emigrant waggon and a forlorn tent, with a camp-fire and a pot, were in the foreground, but there was no trace of the boarding-house, of which I stood a little in dread. The driver went for further directions to the log-cabin, and returned with a grim smile deepening the melancholy of his face to say it was Mr. Chalmers', but there was no accommodation for such as him, much less for me! This was truly " a sell." I got down and found a single room of the rudest kind, with the wall at one end partially broken down, holes in the roof, holes for windows, and no furniture but two chairs and two unplaned wooden

time—my usual resource under discouraging circumstances. I really did not know how I should get on.
There was no table, no bed, no basin, no towel, no
glass, no window, no fastening on the door. The
roof was in holes, the logs were unchinked, and one
end of the cabin was partially removed! Life was
reduced to its simplest elements. I went out; the
family all had something to do, and took no notice
of me. I went back, and then an awkward girl of
sixteen, with uncombed hair, and a painful repulsiveness of face and air, sat on a log for half an hour and
stared at me. I tried to draw her into talk, but she
twirled her fingers and replied snappishly in mono-
syllables. Could I by any effort "make myself
agreeable?" I wondered. The day went on. I put
on my Hawaiian dress, rolling up the sleeves to the
elbows in an "agreeable" fashion. Towards evening
the family returned to feed, and pushed some dried
beef and milk in at the door. They all slept under
the trees, and before dark carried the sacks of straw
out for their bedding. I followed their example
that night, or rather watched Charles's Wain while
they slept, but since then have slept on blankets on
the floor under the roof. They have neither lamp
nor candle, so if I want to do anything after dark I
have to do it by the unsteady light of pine knots.
As the nights are cold, and free from bugs, and I do
a good deal of manual labour, I sleep well. At dusk

I make my bed on the floor, and draw a bucket of
ice-cold water from the river; the family go to sleep
under the trees, and I pile logs on the fire sufficient
to burn half the night, for I assure you the solitude
is *eerie* enough.   There are unaccountable noises,
(wolves), rummagings under the floor, queer cries,
and stealthy sounds of I know not what.   One night
a beast (fox or skunk) rushed in at the open end of
cabin, and fled through the window, almost brushing
my face, and on another, the head and three or four
inches of the body of a snake were protruded through
a chink of the floor close to me, to my extreme dis-
gust.   My mirror is the polished inside of my watch-
case.   At sunrise Mrs. Chalmers comes in—if coming
into a nearly open shed can be called *in*—and makes
a fire, because she thinks me too stupid to do it, and
mine is the family room; and by seven I am dressed,
have folded the blankets, and swept the floor, and
then she puts some milk and bread or stirabout on a
box by the door.   After breakfast I draw more
water, and wash one or two garments daily, taking
care that there are no witnesses of my inexperience.
Yesterday a calf sucked one into hopeless rags.   The
rest of the day I spend in mending, knitting, writing
to you, and the various odds and ends which arise
when one has to do all for oneself.   At twelve and
six some food is put on the box by the door, and at
dusk we make up our beds.   A distressed emigrant

woman has just given birth to a child in a temporary
shanty by the river, and I go to help her each day.
I have made the acquaintance of all the careworn,
struggling settlers within a walk.   All have come
for health, and most have found or are finding it,
even if they have no better shelter than a waggon
tilt or a blanket on sticks laid across four poles.
The climate of Colorado is considered the finest in
North America, and consumptives, asthmatics, dys-
peptics, and sufferers from nervous diseases, are here
in hundreds and thousands, either trying the " camp
cure" for three or four months, or settling here per-
manently.   People can safely sleep out of doors for
six months of the year.   The plains are from 4000
to 6000 feet high, and some of the settled " parks," or
mountain valleys, are from 8000 to 10,000.   The
air, besides being much rarefied, is very dry.   The
rainfall is far below the average, dews are rare, and
fogs nearly unknown.   The sunshine is bright and
almost constant, and three-fourths of the days are
cloudless.   The milk, beef, and bread are good.   The
climate is neither so hot in summer nor so cold in
winter as that of the States, and when the days are
hot the nights are cool.   Snow rarely lies on the
lower ranges, and horses and cattle don't require to
be either fed or housed during the winter.   Of course
the rarefied air quickens respiration.   All this is
from hearsay.[1]   I am not under favourable circum-

[1] The curative effect of the climate of Colorado can hardly be

LETTER V.

A Dateless Day—"Those hands of yours"—A Puritan—Persevering Shiftlessness—The House-Mother—Family Worship—A Grim Sunday—A "Thick-skulled Englishman"—A Morning Call—Another Atmosphere—The Great Lone Land—"Ill Found"—A Log Camp—Bad Footing for Horses—Accidents—Disappointment.

CANYON, *September.*

THE absence of a date shows my predicament. *They* have no newspaper; *I* have no almanack; the father is away for the day, and none of the others can help me, and they look contemptuously upon my desire for information on the subject. The monotony will come to an end to-morrow, for Chalmers offers to be my guide over the mountains to Estes Park, and has persuaded his wife "for once to go for a frolic;" and with much reluctance, many growls at the waste of time, and many apprehensions of danger and loss, she has consented to accompany him. My life has grown less dull from theirs having become more interesting to me, and as I have "made myself agreeable," we are on fairly friendly terms. My first move in the direction of fraternising was, however, snubbed. A few days ago, having finished my own work, I offered to wash up the plates, but Mrs. C., with a look which conveyed more than words, a curl of her nose, and a sneer in her twang, said, "Guess you'll make more work nor you'll do. Those hands of yours" (very brown and coarse they were) "ain't no good; never done nothing, I guess." Then to her awkward daughter: "This woman says she'll wash up! Ha! ha! look at her arms and hands!" This was the nearest approach to a laugh I have heard, and have never seen even a tendency towards a smile. Since then I have risen in their estimation by improvising a lamp—Hawaiian fashion —by putting a wisp of rag into a tin of fat. They have actually condescended to sit up till the stars come out since. Another advance was made by means of the shell-pattern quilt I am knitting for you. There has been a tendency towards approving of it, and a few days since the girl snatched it out of my hand, saying, "I want this," and apparently took it to the camp. This has resulted in my having a knitting-class, with the woman, her married daughter, and a woman from the camp, as pupils. Then I have gained ground with the man by being able to catch and saddle a horse. I am often reminded of my favourite couplet,—

" Beware of desperate steps ; the darkest day,
    Live till to-morrow, will have passed away."

But oh! what a hard, narrow life it is with which I am now in contact! A narrow and unattractive religion, which I believe still to be genuine, and an intense but narrow patriotism, are the only higher influences. Chalmers came from Illinois nine years ago, pronounced by the doctors to be far gone in consumption, and in two years he was strong. They are a queer family; somewhere in the remote Highlands I have seen such another. Its head is tall, gaunt, lean, and ragged, and has lost one eye. On an English road one would think him a starving or a dangerous beggar. He is slightly intelligent, very opinionated, and wishes to be thought well-informed, which he is not. He belongs to the straitest sect of Reformed Presbyterians ("Psalm-singers"), but exaggerates anything of bigotry and intolerance which may characterise them, and rejoices in truly merciless fashion over the excision of the philanthropic Mr. Stuart, of Philadelphia, for worshipping with congregations which sing hymns. His great boast is that his ancestors were Scottish Covenanters. He considers himself a profound theologian, and by the pine logs at night discourses to me on the mysteries of the eternal counsels and the divine decrees. Colorado, with its progress and its future, is also a constant theme. He hates England with a bitter, personal hatred, and regards any allusions which I make to the progress of Victoria as a personal insult. He trusts to live to see the downfall of the British mon-

nothing but the ability to procure the bare necessaries of life.

Of Mrs. C. I can say less. She looks like one of the English poor women of our childhood — lean, clean, toothless, and speaks, like some of them, in a piping, discontented voice, which seems to convey a personal reproach. All her waking hours are spent in a large sun-bonnet. She is never idle for one minute, is severe and hard, and despises everything but work. I think she suffers from her husband's shiftlessness. She always speaks of me as "this" or "that woman." The family consists of a grown-up son, a shiftless, melancholy-looking youth, who possibly pines for a wider life; a girl of sixteen, a sour, repellent-looking creature, with as much manners as a pig; and three hard, unchildlike younger children. By the whole family all courtesy and gentleness of act or speech seem regarded as "works of the flesh," if not of "the devil." They knock over all one's things without apologising or picking them up, and when I thank them for anything they look grimly amazed. I feel that they think it sinful that I do not work as hard as they do. I wish I could show them "a more excellent way." This hard greed, and the exclusive pursuit of gain, with the indifference to all which does not aid in its acquisition, are eating up family love and life throughout the West. I write this reluctantly, and after a total experience of nearly two years in the United States. They seem to have no " Sunday clothes," and few of any kind. The sewing-machine, like most other things, is out of order. One comb serves the whole family. Mrs. C. is cleanly in her person and dress, and the food, though poor, is clean. Work, work, work, is their day and their life. They are thoroughly ungenial, and have that air of suspicion in speaking of every one which is not unusual in the land of their ancestors. Thomas Chalmers is the man's ecclesiastical hero, in spite of his own severe Puritanism. Their live stock consists of two wretched horses, a fairly good *broncho* mare, a mule, four badly-bred cows, four gaunt and famished-looking oxen, some swine of singularly active habits, and plenty of poultry. The old saddles are tied on with twine; one side of the bridle is a worn-out strap and the other a rope. They wear boots, but never two of one pair, and never blacked, of course, but no stockings. They think it quite effeminate to sleep under a roof, except during the severest months of the year. There is a married daughter across the river, just the same hard, love-less, moral, hard-working being as her mother. Each morning, soon after seven, when I have swept the cabin, the family come in for " worship." Chalmers " wales " a psalm, in every sense of the word wail, to the most doleful of dismal tunes ; they read a chapter round, and he prays. If his prayer has something of the tone of the imprecatory psalms, he has high authority in his favour; and if there be a tinge of the Pharisaic thanksgiving, it is hardly surprising that he is grateful that he is not as other men are when he contemplates the general godlessness of the region.

Sunday was a dreadful day. The family kept the Commandment literally, and did no work. Worship was conducted twice, and was rather longer than usual. Chalmers does not allow of any books in his house but theological works, and two or three volumes of dull travels, so the mother and children slept nearly all day. The man attempted to read a well-worn copy of *Boston's Fourfold State*, but shortly fell asleep, and they only woke up for their meals. Friday and Saturday had been passably cool, with frosty nights, but on Saturday night it changed, and I have not felt anything like the heat of Sunday since I left New Zealand, though the mercury was not higher than 91°. It was sickening, scorching, melting, unbearable, from the mere power of the sun's rays. It was an awful day, and seemed as if it would never come to an end. The cabin, with its mud roof under the shade of the trees, gave a little shelter, but it was occupied by the family, and I longed for solitude. I took the *Imitation of Christ*, and strolled up the canyon among the withered, crackling leaves, in much dread of snakes, and lay down on a rough table which some passing emigrant

beautified, grinding life. These people live in a discomfort and lack of ease and refinement which seems only possible to people of British stock. A "foreigner" fills his cabin with ingenuities and elegancies, and a Hawaiian or South Sea Islander makes his grass house both pretty and tasteful. Add to my surroundings a mighty canyon, impassable both above and below, and walls of mountains with an opening some miles off to the vast prairie sea.[1]

An English physician is settled about half a mile from here over a hill. He is spoken off as holding "very extreme opinions." Chalmers rails at him for being "a thick-skulled Englishman," for being "fine, polished," etc. To say a man is "polished" here is to give him a very bad name. He accuses him also of holding views subversive of all morality. In spite of all this, I thought he might possess a map, and I induced Mrs. C. to walk over with me. She intended it as a formal morning call, but she wore the inevitable sun-bonnet, and had her dress tied up as when washing. It was not till I reached the gate that I remembered that I was in my Hawaiian riding-dress, and that I still wore the spurs with which I had been trying a horse in the morning! The house was in a

[1] I have not curtailed this description of the roughness of a Colorado settler's life, for, with the exceptions of the disrepair and the Puritanism, it is a type of the hard, unornamented existence with which I came almost universally in contact during my subsequent residence in the Territory.

grass valley which opened from the tremendous
canyon through which the river had cut its way.
The Foot Hills, with their terraces of flaming red
rock, were glowing in the sunset, and a pure green
sky arched tenderly over a soft evening scene. Used
to the meanness and baldness of settlers' dwellings,
I was delighted to see that in this instance the usual
log cabin was only the lower floor of a small house,
which bore a delightful resemblance to a Swiss châlet.
It stood in a vegetable garden fertilised by an irrigating ditch, outside of which were a barn and cowshed.
A young Swiss girl was bringing the cows slowly
home from the hill, an Englishwoman in a clean print
dress stood by the fence holding a baby, and a fine-
looking Englishman in a striped Garibaldi shirt, and
trousers of the same tucked into high boots, was
shelling corn. As soon as Mrs. Hughes spoke I felt
she was truly a lady; and oh! how refreshing her
refined, courteous, graceful English manner was, as
she invited us into the house! The entrance was
low, through a log porch festooned and almost concealed by a "wild cucumber." Inside, though plain
and poor, the room looked a home, not like a
squatter's cabin. An old tin was completely covered
by a graceful clematis mixed with streamers of Virginia creeper, and white muslin curtains, and above
all two shelves of admirably-chosen books, gave the
room almost an air of elegance. Why do I write

almost? It was an oasis. It was barely three
weeks since I had left "the communion of educated
men," and the first tones of the voices of my host
and hostess made me feel as if I had been out of it
for a year. Mrs. C. stayed an hour and a half, and
then went home to the cows, when we launched upon
a sea of congenial talk. They said they had not seen
an educated lady for two years, and pressed me to go
and visit them. I rode home on Dr. Hughes's horse
after dark, to find neither fire nor light in the cabin.
Mrs. C. had gone back saying, "Those English talked
just like savages, I couldn't understand a word they
said." I made a fire, and extemporised a light with
some fat and a wick of rag, and Chalmers came in to
discuss my visit and to ask me a question concerning
a matter which had roused the latent curiosity of the
whole family. I had told him, he said, that I knew no
one hereabouts, but "his woman" told him that Dr.
H. and I spoke constantly of a Mrs. Grundy, whom
we both knew and disliked, and who was settled, as
we said, not far off! He had never heard of her, he
said, and he was the pioneer settler of the canyon,
and there was a man up here from Longmount who
said he was sure there was not a Mrs. Grundy in the
district, unless it was a woman who went by two
names! The wife and family had then come in, and I
felt completely nonplussed. I longed to tell Chalmers
that it was he and such as he, there or anywhere,

at me, and then quietly trotted away. He was so near that I heard the grass, crisp with hoar frost, crackle under his feet. Bears stripped the cherry-bushes within a few yards of us last night. Now two lovely blue birds, with crests on their heads, are picking about within a stone's-throw. This is "The Great Lone Land," until lately the hunting-ground of the Indians, and not yet settled or traversed, or likely to be so, owing to the want of water. A solitary hunter has built a log cabin up here, which he occupies for a few weeks for the purpose of elk-hunting, but all the region is unsurveyed, and mostly unexplored. It is 7 A.M. The sun has not yet risen high enough to melt the hoar-frost, and the air is clear, bright, and cold. The stillness is profound. I hear nothing but the far-off mysterious roaring of a river in a deep canyon, which we spent two hours last night in trying to find. The horses are lost, and if I were disposed to retort upon my companions the term they invariably apply to me, I should now write, with bitter emphasis, "*that* man" and "*that* woman" have gone in search of them.

The scenery up here is glorious, combining sublimity with beauty, and in the elastic air fatigue has dropped off from me. This is no region for tourists and women, only for a few elk and bear hunters at times, and its unprofaned freshness gives me new life. I cannot by any words give you an idea of scenery so different from any that you or I have ever seen. This is an upland valley of grass and flowers, of glades and sloping lawns, and cherry-fringed beds of dry streams, and clumps of pines artistically placed, and mountain sides densely pine-clad, the pines breaking into fringes as they come down upon the "park," and the mountains breaking into pinnacles of bold grey rock as they pierce the blue of the sky. A single dell of bright green grass, on which dwarf clumps of the scarlet poison-oak look like beds of geraniums, slopes towards the west, as if it must lead to the river which we seek. Deep, vast canyons, all trending westwards, lie in purple gloom. Pine-clad ranges, rising into the blasted top of Storm Peak, all run westwards too, and all the beauty and glory are but the frame out of which rises—heaven-piercing, pure in its pearly lustre, as glorious a mountain as the sun tinges red in either hemisphere —the splintered, pinnacled, lonely, ghastly, impos-ing, double-peaked summit of Long's Peak, the Mont Blanc of Northern Colorado.[1]

This is a view to which nothing needs to be added. This is truly the "lodge in some vast wil-derness" for which one often sighs when in the midst

[1] Gray's Peak and Pike's Peak have their partisans, but after seeing them all under favourable aspects, Long's Peak stands in my memory as it does in that vast congeries of mountains, alone in imperial grandeur.

of " a bustle at once sordid and trivial." In spite of
Dr. Johnson, these "monstrous protuberances" do
"inflame the imagination and elevate the understanding." This scenery satisfies my soul. Now, the
Rocky Mountains realise—nay, exceed—the dream
of my childhood. It is magnificent, and the air is
life-giving. I should like to spend some time in
these higher regions, but I know that this will turn
out an abortive expedition, owing to the stupidity
and pigheadedness of Chalmers.

There is a most romantic place called Estes Park,
at a height of 7500 feet, which can be reached by
going down to the plains and then striking up the
St. Vrain Canyon, but this is a distance of 55 miles,
and as Chalmers was confident that he could take
me over the mountains, a distance, as he supposed,
of about 20 miles, we left at mid-day yesterday,
with the fervent hope, on my part, that I might
not return. Mrs. C. was busy the whole of Tuesday
in preparing what she called "grub," which, together
with "plenty of bedding," was to be carried on a
pack mule; but when we started I was disgusted to
find that Chalmers was on what should have been
the pack animal, and that two thickly-quilted cotton
"spreads" had been disposed of under my saddle,
making it broad, high, and uncomfortable. Any
human being must have laughed to see an expedition start so grotesquely " ill found." I had a very

old iron-grey horse, whose lower lip hung down feebly, showing his few teeth, while his fore-legs stuck out forwards, and matter ran from both his nearly-blind eyes. It is a kindness to bring him up to abundant pasture. My saddle is an old McLellan cavalry saddle, with a battered brass peak, and the bridle is a rotten leather strap on one side and a strand of rope on the other. The cotton quilts covered the Rosinante from mane to tail. Mrs. C. wore an old print skirt, an old short-gown, a print apron, and a sun-bonnet, with the flap coming down to her waist, and looked as careworn and clean as she always does. The inside horn of her saddle was broken; to the outside one hung a saucepan and a bundle of clothes. The one girth was nearly at the breaking-point when we started.

My pack, with my well-worn umbrella upon it, was behind my saddle. I wore my Hawaiian riding-dress, with a handkerchief tied over my face and the sun-cover of my umbrella folded and tied over my hat, for the sun was very fierce. The queerest figure of all was the would-be guide. With his one eye, his gaunt, lean form, and his torn clothes, he looked more like a strolling tinker than the honest worthy settler that he is. He bestrode rather than rode a gaunt mule, whose tail hair had all been shaven off, except a tuft for a tassel at the end. Two flour bags which leaked were tied on behind the saddle, two quilts were under it, and my canvas bag, a battered canteen, a frying-pan, and two lariats hung from the horn. On one foot C. wore an old high boot, into which his trouser was tucked, and on the other an old brogue, through which his toes protruded.

We had an ascent of four hours through a ravine which gradually opened out upon this beautiful " park," but we rode through it for some miles before the view burst upon us. The vastness of this range, like astronomical distances, can hardly be conceived of. At this place, I suppose, it is not less than 250 miles wide, and with hardly a break in its continuity, it stretches almost from the Arctic circle to the Straits of Magellan. From the top of Long's Peak, within a short distance, twenty-two summits, each above 12,000 feet in height, are visible, and the Snowy Range, the backbone or " divide " of the continent, is seen snaking distinctly through the wilderness of ranges, with its waters starting for either ocean. From the first ridge we crossed after leaving Canyon we had a singular view of range beyond range cleft by deep canyons, and abounding in elliptical valleys, richly grassed. The slopes of all the hills, as far as one could see, were waving with fine grass ready for the scythe, but the food of wild animals only. All these ridges are heavily timbered with pitch pines, and where they come down on the grassy slopes they look as if the trees

had been arranged by a landscape gardener. Far
off, through an opening in a canyon, we saw the
prairie simulating the ocean. Far off, through an
opening in another direction, was the glistening out-
line of the Snowy Range. But still, till we reached
this place, it was monotonous, though grand as a
whole : a grey-green or buff-grey, with outbreaks of
brilliantly-coloured rock, only varied by the black
green of pines, which are not the stately pyramidal
pines of the Sierra Nevada, but much resemble the
natural Scotch fir. Not many miles from us is North
Park, a great tract of land said to be rich in gold,
but those who have gone to " prospect " have seldom
returned, the region being the home of tribes of
Indians who live in perpetual hostility to the whites
and to each other.

At this great height, and most artistically situated,
we came upon a rude log camp tenanted in winter by
an elk hunter, but now deserted. Chalmers without
any scruple picked the padlock ; we lighted a fire,
made some tea, and fried some bacon, and after a
good meal mounted again and started for Estes Park.
For four weary hours we searched hither and thither
along every indentation of the ground which might
be supposed to slope towards the Big Thompson
River, which we knew had to be forded. Still, as
the quest grew more tedious, Long's Peak stood before us as a landmark in purple glory; and still at

his feet lay a hollow filled with deep blue atmosphere, where I knew that Estes Park must lie, and still between us and it lay never-lessening miles of inaccessibility, and the sun was ever westering, and the shadows ever lengthening, and Chalmers, who had started confident, bumptious, blatant, was ever becoming more bewildered, and his wife's thin voice more piping and discontented, and my stumbling horse more insecure, and I more determined (as I am at this moment) that somehow or other I would reach that blue hollow, and even stand on Long's Peak where the snow was glittering. Affairs were becoming serious, and Chalmers's incompetence a source of real peril, when, after an exploring expedition, he returned more bumptious than ever, saying he knew it would be all right, he had found a trail, and we could get across the river by dark, and camp out for the night. So he led us into a steep, deep, rough ravine, where we had to dismount, for trees were lying across it everywhere, and there was almost no footing on the great slabs of shelving rock. Yet there was a trail, tolerably well worn, and the branches and twigs near the ground were well broken back. Ah! it was a wild place. My horse fell first, rolling over twice, and breaking off a part of the saddle, in his second roll knocking me over a shelf of three feet of descent. Then Mrs C.'s horse and the mule fell on the top of each other, and on recovering them-

had no food, but made a fire. I lay down on some
dry grass, with my inverted saddle for a pillow, and
slept soundly, till I was awoke by the cold of an
intense frost, and the pain of my many cuts and
bruises. Chalmers promised that we should make a
fresh start at six, so I woke him at five, and here I
am alone at half-past eight! I said to him many
times that unless he hobbled or picketed the horses,
we should lose them. "Oh," he said, "they'll be all
right." In truth he had no picketing-pins. Now,
the animals are merrily trotting homewards. I saw
them two miles off an hour ago with him after them.
His wife, who is also after them, goaded to desperation, said, "He's the most ignorant, careless, good-for-
nothing man I ever saw," upon which I dwelt upon
his being well-meaning. There is a sort of well here,
but our "afternoon tea" and watering the horses
drained it, so we have had nothing to drink since
yesterday, for the canteen, which started without a
cork, lost all its contents when the mule fell. I have
made a monstrous fire, but thirst and impatience are
hard to bear, and preventible misfortunes are always
irksome. I have found the stomach of a bear with
fully a pint of cherrystones in it, and have spent an
hour in getting the kernels; and lo! now, at half-
past nine, I see the culprit and his wife coming back
with the animals!

I. L. B.

LOWER CANYON, *September 21.*

We never reached Estes Park. There is no trail, and horses have never been across. We started from camp at ten, and spent four hours in searching for the trail. Chalmers tried gulch after gulch again, his self-assertion giving way a little after each failure; sometimes going east when we should have gone west, always being brought up by a precipice or other impossibility. At last he went off by himself, and returned rejoicing, saying he had found the trail; and soon, sure enough, we were on a well-defined old trail, evidently made by carcasses which have been dragged along it by hunters. Vainly I pointed out to him that we were going north-east when we should have gone south-west, and that we were ascending instead of descending. " Oh, it's all right, and we shall soon come to water," he always replied. For two hours we ascended slowly through a thicket of aspen, the cold continually intensifying; but the trail, which had been growing fainter, died out, and an opening showed the top of Storm Peak not far off and not much above us, though it is 11,000 feet high. I could not help laughing. He had deliberately turned his back on Estes Park. He then confessed that he was lost, and that he could not find the way back. His wife sat down on the ground and cried bitterly. We ate some dry bread, and then I said I had had much experience in travelling, and would take the control of the party, which was agreed to, and we began the long descent. Soon after his wife was thrown from her horse, and cried bitterly again from fright and mortification. Soon after that the girth of the mule's saddle broke, and having no crupper, saddle and addenda went over his head, and the flour was dispersed. Next the girth of the woman's saddle broke, and she went over her horse's head. Then he began to fumble helplessly at it, railing against England the whole time, while I secured the saddle, and guided the route back to an outlet of the park. There a fire was built, and we had some bread and bacon; and then a search for water occupied nearly two hours, and resulted in the finding of a mud-hole, trodden and defiled by hundreds of feet of elk, bears, cats, deer, and other beasts, and containing only a few gallons of water as thick as pea-soup, with which we watered our animals and made some strong tea.

The sun was setting in glory as we started for the four hours' ride home, and the frost was intense, and made our bruised, grazed limbs ache painfully. I was sorry for Mrs. Chalmers, who had had several falls, and bore her aches patiently, and had said several times to her husband, with a kind meaning, " I am real sorry for this woman." I was so tired with the perpetual stumbling of my horse, as well as stiffened

LETTER VI.

A *bronco* Mare—An Accident—Wonderland—A Sad Story—The
Children of the Territories—Hard Greed—Halcyon Hours—
Smartness—Old-fashioned Prejudices—The Chicago Colony—
Good luck—Three Notes of Admiration—A good Horse—The
St. Vrain—The Rocky Mountains at last—" Mountain Jim"—A
death hug—Estes Park.

LOWER CANYON, *September 25.*

THIS is another world.   My entrance upon it was sig-
nalised in this fashion.   Chalmers offered me a *bronco*
mare for a reasonable sum, and though she was a shifty,
half-broken young thing, I came over here on her to
try her, when, just as I was going away, she took into
her head to " scare" and " buck," and when I touched
her with my foot she leaped over a heap of timber,
and the girth gave way, and the onlookers tell me
that while she jumped I fell over her tail from a good
height upon the hard gravel, receiving a parting kick
on my knee.   They could hardly believe that no bones
were broken.   The flesh of my left arm looks crushed
into a jelly, but cold-water dressings will soon bring
it right; and a cut on my back bled profusely; and
the bleeding, with many bruises and the general
shake, have made me feel weak, but circumstances

do not admit of "making a fuss," and I really think that the rents in my riding-dress will prove the most important part of the accident.

The surroundings here are pleasing. The log cabin, on the top of which a room with a steep, ornamental Swiss roof has been built, is in a valley close to a clear, rushing river, which emerges a little higher up from an inaccessible chasm of great sublimity. One side of the valley is formed by cliffs and terraces of porphyry as red as the reddest new brick, and at sunset blazing into vermilion. Through rifts in the nearer ranges there are glimpses of pine-clothed peaks, which, towards twilight, pass through every shade of purple and violet. The sky and the earth combine to form a Wonderland every evening—such rich, velvety colouring in crimson and violet; such an orange, green, and vermilion sky; such scarlet and emerald clouds; such an extraordinary dryness and purity of atmosphere, and then the glorious afterglow which seems to blend earth and heaven! For colour, the Rocky Mountains beat all I have seen. The air has been cold, but the sun bright and hot during the last few days.

The story of my host is a story of misfortune. It indicates who should *not* come to Colorado.[1] He and

[1] The story is ended now. A few months after my visit Mrs. H. died a few days after her confinement, and was buried on the bleak hill-side, leaving her husband with five children under six years old, and Dr. H. is a prosperous man on one of the sunniest islands of the Pacific, with the devoted Swiss friend as his second wife.

his wife are under thirty-five. The son of a London
physician in large practice, with a liberal education
in the largest sense of the word, unusual culture and
accomplishments, and the partner of a physician in
good practice in the second city in England, he showed
symptoms which threatened pulmonary disease. In
an evil hour he heard of Colorado with its " unrivalled climate, boundless resources," etc., and, fas-
cinated not only by these material advantages, but
by the notion of being able to found or reform society
on advanced social theories of his own, he became an
emigrant. Mrs. Hughes is one of the most charming,
cultured, and lovable women I have ever seen, and
their marriage is an ideal one. Both are fitted to
shine in any society, but neither had the slightest
knowledge of domestic and farming details. Dr. H.
did not know how to saddle or harness a horse. Mrs.
H. did not know whether you should put an egg into
cold or hot water when you meant to boil it ! They
arrived at Longmount, bought up this claim, rather
for the beauty of the scenery than for any substantial
advantages, were cheated in land, goods, oxen, everything, and, to the discredit of the settlers, seemed to be
regarded as fair game. Everything has failed with
them, and though they " rise early, and late take rest,
and eat the bread of carefulness," they hardly keep
their heads above water. A young Swiss girl, devoted
to them both, works as hard as they do. They have

difficulties has already told on these infants. They consider their mother in all things, going without butter when they think the stock is low, bringing in wood and water too heavy for them to carry, anxiously speculating on the winter prospect and the crops, yet withal the most childlike and innocent of children.

One of the most painful things in the Western States and Territories is the extinction of childhood. I have never seen any children, only debased imitations of men and women, cankered by greed and selfishness, and asserting and gaining complete independence of their parents at ten years old. The atmosphere in which they are brought up is one of greed, godlessness, and frequently of profanity. Consequently these sweet things seem like flowers in a desert.

Except for love, which here as everywhere raises life into the ideal, this is a wretched existence. The poor crops have been destroyed by grasshoppers over and over again, and that talent deified here under the name of " smartness" has taken advantage of Dr. H. in all bargains, leaving him with little except food for his children. Experience has been dearly bought in all ways, and this instance of failure might be a useful warning to professional men without agricultural experience not to come and try to make a living by farming in Colorado.

My time here has passed very delightfully in spite of my regret and anxiety for this interesting family.

I should like to stay longer, were it not that they have given up to me their straw bed, and Mrs. H. and her baby, a wizened, fretful child, sleep on the floor in my room, and Dr. H. on the floor downstairs, and the nights are frosty and chill. Work is the order of their day, and of mine, and at night, when the children are in bed, we three ladies patch the clothes and make shirts, and Dr. H. reads Tennyson's poems, or we speak tenderly of that world of culture and noble deeds which seems here "the land very far off," or Mrs. H. lays aside her work for a few minutes and reads some favourite passage of prose or poetry, as I have seldom heard either read before, with a voice of large compass and exquisite tone, quick to interpret every shade of the author's meaning, and soft, speaking eyes, moist with feeling and sympathy. These are our halcyon hours, when we forget the needs of the morrow, and that men still buy, sell, cheat, and strive for gold, and that we are in the Rocky Mountains, and that it is near midnight. But morning comes hot and tiresome, and the never-ending work is oppressive, and Dr. H. comes in from the field two or three times in the day, dizzy and faint, and they condole with each other, and I feel that the Colorado settler needs to be made of sterner stuff and to possess more adaptability.

To-day has been a very pleasant day for me, though I have only once sat down since 9 A.M., and

it is now 5 P.M.   I plotted that the devoted Swiss girl
should go to the nearest settlement with two of the
children for the day in a neighbour's waggon, and
that Dr. and Mrs. H. should get an afternoon of rest
and sleep upstairs, while I undertook to do the work
and make something of a cleaning. I had a large
" wash" of my own, having been hindered last week
by my bad arm, but a clothes-wringer which screws
on to the side of the tub is a great assistance, and by
folding the clothes before passing them through it, I
make it serve instead of mangle and iron. After
baking the bread and thoroughly cleaning the churn
and pails, I began upon the tins and pans, the cleaning of which had fallen into arrears, and was hard at
work, very greasy and grimy, when a man came in to
know where to ford the river with his ox-team, and
as I was showing him he looked pityingly at me,
saying, " Be you the new hired girl? Bless me,
you're awful small!"

Yesterday we saved three cwt. of tomatoes for
winter use, and about two tons of squash and pump-
kin for the cattle, two of the former weighing 140
lbs. I pulled nearly a quarter of an acre of maize,
but it was a scanty crop, and the husks were poorly
filled. I much prefer field work to the scouring of
greasy pans and to the wash-tub, and both to either
sewing or writing.

This is not Arcadia. " Smartness," which consists in over-reaching your neighbour in every fashion which is not illegal, is the quality which is held in the greatest repute, and Mammon is the divinity. From a generation brought up to worship the one and admire the other little can be hoped. In districts distant as this is from " Church Ordinances," there are three ways in which Sunday is spent: one, to make it a day for visiting, hunting, and fishing; another, to spend it in sleeping and abstinence from work; and the third, to continue all the usual occupations, consequently harvesting and felling and hauling timber are to be seen in progress. Last Sunday a man came here and put up a door, and said he didn't believe in the Bible or in a God, and he wasn't going to sacrifice his children's bread to old-fashioned prejudices. There is a manifest indifference to the higher obligations of the law, "judgment, mercy, and faith;" but in the main the settlers are steady, there are few flagrant breaches of morals, industry is the rule, life and property are far safer than in England or Scotland, and the law of universal respect to women is still in full force.

The days are now brilliant and the nights sharply frosty. People are preparing for the winter. The tourists from the east are trooping into Denver, and the surveying parties are coming down from the mountains. Snow has fallen on the higher ranges, and my hopes of getting to Estes Park are down at zero.

LONGMOUNT, *September 25.*

Yesterday was perfect. The sun was brilliant and the air cool and bracing. I felt better, and after a hard day's work and an evening stroll with my friends in the glorious afterglow, I went to bed cheerful and hopeful as to the climate and its effect on my health. This morning I awoke with a sensation of extreme lassitude, and on going out, instead of the delicious atmosphere of yesterday, I found intolerable suffocating heat, a *blazing* (not *brilliant*) sun, and a sirocco like a Victorian hot wind. Neuralgia, inflamed eyes, and a sense of extreme prostration followed, and my acclimatised hosts were somewhat similarly affected. The sparkle, the crystalline atmosphere, and the glory of colour of yesterday, had all vanished. We had borrowed a waggon, but Dr. H.'s strong but lazy horse and a feeble hired one made a poor span; and though the distance here is only twenty-two miles over level prairie, our tired animal, and losing the way three times, have kept us eight and a half hours in the broiling sun. All notions of locality fail me on the prairie, and Dr. H. was not much better. We took wrong tracks, got entangled among fences, plunged through the deep mud of irrigation ditches, and were despondent. It was a miserable drive, sitting on a heap of fodder under the angry sun. Half-way here we camped at a river, now only a series of mud-holes, and I fell asleep under the im-

perfect shade of a cotton-wood tree, dreading the
thought of waking and jolting painfully along over
the dusty prairie in the dust-laden, fierce sirocco,
under the ferocious sun. We never saw man or
beast the whole day.

This is the " Chicago Colony," and it is said to be
prospering, after some preliminary land swindles. It
is as uninviting as Fort Collins. We first came upon
dust-coloured frame-houses set down at intervals on
the dusty buff plain, each with its dusty wheat or
barley field adjacent, the crop, not the product of the
rains of heaven, but of the muddy overflow of " Irrigating Ditch No. 2." Then comes a road made up of
many converging waggon tracks, which stiffen into
a wide straggling street, in which glaring frame-
houses and a few shops stand opposite to each other.
A two-storey house, one of the whitest and most
glaring, and without a verandah like all the others,
is the " St. Vrain Hotel," called after the St. Vrain
river, out of which the ditch is taken which enables
Longmount to exist. Everything was broiling in the
heat of the slanting sun, which all day long had been
beating on the unshaded wooden rooms. The heat
within was more sickening than outside, and black
flies covered everything, one's face included. We all
sat fighting the flies in my bedroom, which was
cooler than elsewhere, till a glorious sunset over the
Rocky Range, some ten miles off, compelled us to go

out and enjoy it. Then followed supper, Western fashion, without table-cloths, and all the "unattached" men of Longmount came in and fed silently and rapidly. It was a great treat to have tea to drink, as I had not tasted any for a fortnight. The landlord is a jovial, kindly man. I told him how my plans had failed, and how I was reluctantly going on to-morrow to Denver and New York, being unable to get to Estes Park, and he said there might yet be a chance of some one coming in to-night who would be going up. He soon came to my room and asked definitely what I could do—if I feared cold, if I could "rough it," if I could "ride horseback and lope." Estes Park and its surroundings are, he says, "the most beautiful scenery in Colorado," and "it's a real shame," he added, "for you not to see it." We had hardly sat down to tea when he came, saying, "You're in luck this time; two young men have just come in and are going up to-morrow morning." I am rather pleased, and have hired a horse for three days; but I am not very hopeful, for I am almost ill of the smothering heat, and still suffer from my fall, and not having been on horseback since, twenty-five and a half miles will be a long ride. Then I fear that the accommodation is as rough as Chalmers's, and that solitude will be impossible. We have been strolling in the street ever since it grew dark to get the little air which is moving.

ESTES PARK ! ! ! *September 28.*

I wish I could let those three notes of admiration go to you instead of a letter. They mean everything that is rapturous and delightful—grandeur, cheerfulness, health, enjoyment, novelty, freedom, etc. etc. I have just dropped into the very place I have been seeking, but in everything it exceeds all my dreams. There is health in every breath of air; I am much better already, and get up to a seven o'clock breakfast without difficulty. It is quite comfortable—in the fashion that I like. I have a log cabin, raised on six posts, all to myself, with a skunk's lair underneath it, and a small lake close to it. There is a frost every night, and all day it is cool enough for a roaring fire. The ranchman, who is half hunter half stockman, and his wife are jovial, hearty Welsh people from Llanberis, who laugh with loud, cheery British laughs, sing in parts down to the youngest child, are freehearted and hospitable, and pile the pitch-pine logs half-way up the great rude chimney. There has been fresh meat each day since I came, delicious bread baked daily, excellent potatoes, tea and coffee, and an abundant supply of milk like cream. I have a clean hay bed with six blankets, and there are neither bugs nor fleas. The scenery is the most glorious I have ever seen, and is above us, around us, at the very door. Most people have advised me to go to Colorado Springs, and only one mentioned this place, and till I reached Longmount I never saw any one who had been here, but I saw from the lie of the country that it must be most superbly situated. People said, however, that it was most difficult of access, and that the season for it was over. In travelling there is nothing like dissecting people's statements, which are usually coloured by their estimate of the powers or likings of the person spoken to, making all reasonable inquiries, and then pertinaciously but quietly carrying out one's own plans. This is perfection, and all the requisites for health are present, including plenty of horses and grass to ride on.

It is not easy to sit down to write after ten hours of hard riding, especially in a cabin full of people, and wholesome fatigue may make my letter flat when it ought to be enthusiastic. I was awake all night at Longmount owing to the stifling heat, and got up nervous and miserable, ready to give up the thought of coming here, but the sunrise over the plains, and the wonderful red of the Rocky Mountains, as they reflected the eastern sky, put spirit into me. The landlord had got a horse, but could not give any satisfactory assurances of his being quiet, and being much shaken by my fall at Canyon, I earnestly wished that the *Greeley Tribune* had not given me a reputation for horsemanship, which had preceded me here. The young men who were to escort me "seemed very innocent," he said, but I have not arrived at his meaning yet. When the horse appeared in the street at 8.30, I saw, to my dismay, a high-bred, beautiful creature, stable-kept, with arched neck, quivering nostrils, and restless ears and eyes. My pack, as on Hawaii, was strapped behind the Mexican saddle, and my canvas bag hung on the horn, but the horse did not look fit to carry "gear," and seemed to require two men to hold and coax him. There were many loafers about, and I shrank from going out and mounting in my old Hawaiian riding-dress, though Dr. and Mrs. H. assured me that I looked quite "insignificant and unnoticeable." We got away at nine with repeated injunctions from the landlord in the words, "Oh, you should be heroic!"

The sky was cloudless, and a deep brilliant blue, and though the sun was hot the air was fresh and bracing. The ride for glory and delight I shall label along with one to Hanalei, and another to Mauna Kea, Hawaii. I felt better quite soon; the horse in gait and temper turned out perfection—all spring and spirit, elastic in his motion, walking fast and easily, and cantering with a light, graceful swing as soon as one pressed the reins on his neck, a blithe, joyous animal, to whom a day among the mountains seemed a pleasant frolic. So gentle he was, that when I got off and walked he followed me without being led, and without needing any one to hold him he allowed me to mount on either side. In addition to the charm of his movements he has the cat-like sure-footedness of a Hawaiian horse, and fords rapid and rough-bottomed rivers, and gallops among stones and stumps, and down steep hills, with equal security. I could have ridden him a hundred miles as easily as twenty-five and a half. We have only been together two days, yet we are firm friends, and thoroughly understand each other. I should not require another companion on a long mountain tour. All his ways are those of an animal brought up without curb, whip, or spur, trained by the voice, and used only to kindness, as is happily the case with the majority of horses in the Western States. Consequently, unless they are *broncos*, they exercise their intelligence for your advantage, and do their work rather as friends than as machines.

I soon began not only to feel better, but to be exhilarated with the delightful motion. The sun was behind us, and puffs of a cool elastic air came down from the glorious mountains in front. We cantered across six miles of prairie, and then reached the beautiful canyon of the St. Vrain, which, towards its mouth, is a narrow, fertile, wooded valley, through which a bright rapid river, which we forded many times, hurries along, with twists and windings innumerable. Ah, how brightly its ripples danced in the glittering sunshine, and how musically its waters murmured like the streams of windward Hawaii! We lost our way over and over again, though the "innocent" young men had been there before; indeed, it would require some talent to master the intricacies of that devious trail, but settlers making hay always appeared in the nick of time to put us on the right track. Very fair it was, after the brown and burning plains, and the variety was endless. Cotton-wood trees were green and bright, aspens shivered in golden tremulousness, wild grape-vines trailed their lemon-coloured foliage along the ground, and the Virginia creeper hung its crimson sprays here and there, lighting up green and gold into glory. Sometimes from under the cool and bowery shade of the coloured tangle we passed into the cool St. Vrain, and then were wedged between its margin and lofty cliffs and terraces of incredibly staring, fantastic rocks, lined, patched, and splashed with carmine, vermilion, greens of all tints, blue, yellow, orange, violet, deep crimson, colouring that no artist would dare to represent, and of which, in sober prose, I scarcely dare tell. Long's wonderful peaks, which hitherto had gleamed above the green, now disappeared, to be seen no more for twenty miles. We entered on an ascending valley, where the gorgeous hues of the rocks were intensified by the blue gloom of the pitch-pines, and then taking a track to the north-west, we left the softer world behind, and all traces of man and his works, and plunged into the Rocky Mountains.

There were wonderful ascents then up which I

led my horse : wild fantastic views opening up continually, a recurrence of surprises; the air keener
and purer with every mile, the sensation of loneliness
more singular. A tremendous ascent among rocks
and pines to a height of 9000 feet brought us to a
passage seven feet wide through a wall of rock, with
an abrupt descent of 2000 feet, and a yet higher
ascent beyond. I never saw anything so strange as
looking back. It was a single gigantic ridge which
we had passed through, standing up knife-like, built
up entirely of great brick-shaped masses of bright-
red rock, some of them as large as the Royal Insti-
tution, Edinburgh, piled one on another by Titans.
Pitch-pines grew out of their crevices, but there was
not a vestige of soil. Beyond, wall beyond wall of
similar construction, and range above range, rose into
the blue sky. Fifteen miles more over great ridges,
along passes dark with shadow, and so narrow that
we had to ride in the beds of the streams which had
excavated them, round the bases of colossal pyramids
of rock crested with pines, up into fair upland
"parks," scarlet in patches with the poison oak,
parks so beautifully arranged by nature that I
momentarily expected to come upon some stately
mansion, but that afternoon crested blue jays and
chipmonks had them all to themselves. Here, in
the early morning, deer, bighorn, and the stately elk,
come down to feed, and there, in the night, prowl

and growl the Rocky Mountain lion, the grizzly
bear, and the cowardly wolf. There were chasms
of immense depth, dark with the indigo gloom of
pines, and mountains with snow gleaming on their
splintered crests, loveliness to bewilder and grandeur
to awe, and still streams and shady pools, and cool
depths of shadow; mountains again, dense with pines,
among which patches of aspen gleamed like gold;
valleys where the yellow cottonwood mingled with
the crimson oak, and so, on and on through the
lengthening shadows, till the trail, which in places
had been hardly legible, became well defined, and
we entered a long gulch with broad swellings of
grass belted with pines.

A very pretty mare, hobbled, was feeding; a
collie dog barked at us, and among the scrub, not far
from the track, there was a rude, black log cabin, as
rough as it could be to be a shelter at all, with smoke
coming out of the roof and window. We diverged
towards it; it mattered not that it was the home, or
rather den, of a notorious "ruffian" and "desperado."
One of my companions had disappeared hours before,
the remaining one was a town-bred youth. I longed
to speak to some one who loved the mountains. I
called the hut a *den*—it looked like the den of a
wild beast. The big dog lay outside it in a threatening attitude and growled. The mud roof was covered
with lynx, beaver, and other furs laid out to dry,

beaver paws were pinned out on the logs, a part of the carcass of a deer hung at one end of the cabin, a skinned beaver lay in front of a heap of peltry just within the door, and antlers of deer, old horseshoes, and offal of many animals, lay about the den. Roused by the growling of the dog, his owner came out, a broad, thickset man, about the middle height, with an old cap on his head, and wearing a grey hunting-suit much the worse for wear (almost falling to pieces, in fact), a digger's scarf knotted round his waist, a knife in his belt, and "a bosom friend," a revolver, sticking out of the breast-pocket of his coat; his feet, which were very small, were bare, except for some dilapidated moccasins made of horse hide. The marvel was how his clothes hung together, and on him. The scarf round his waist must have had something to do with it. His face was remarkable. He is a man about forty-five, and must have been strikingly handsome. He has large grey-blue eyes, deeply set, with well-marked eyebrows, a handsome aquiline nose, and a very handsome mouth. His face was smooth-shaven except for a dense moustache and imperial. Tawny hair, in thin uncared-for curls, fell from under his hunter's cap and over his collar. One eye was entirely gone, and the loss made one side of the face repulsive, while the other might have been modelled in marble. "Desperado" was written in large letters all over him. I almost repented of

man, known through the Territories and beyond them as " Rocky Mountain Jim," or, more briefly, as " Mountain Jim," is one of the famous scouts of the Plains, and is the original of some daring portraits in fiction concerning Indian frontier warfare.   So far as I have at present heard, he is a man for whom there is now no room, for the time for blows and blood in this part of Colorado is past, and the fame of many daring exploits is sullied by crimes which are not easily forgiven here.   He now has a "squatter's claim," but makes his living as a trapper, and is a complete child of the mountains.   Of his genius and chivalry to women there does not appear to be any doubt; but he is a desperate character, and is subject to "ugly fits," when people think it best to avoid him.   It is here regarded as an evil that he has located himself at the mouth of the only entrance to the Park, for he is dangerous with his pistols, and it would be safer if he were not here.   His besetting sin is indicated in the verdict pronounced on him by my host: " When he's sober Jim's a perfect gentleman; but when he's had liquor he's the most awful ruffian in Colorado."

one. But in my intercourse with him I saw more of his nobler instincts than of the darker parts of his character, which, unfortunately for himself and others, showed itself in its worst colours at the time of his tragic end.   It was not until after I left Colorado, not indeed until after his death, that I heard of the worst points of his character.

From the ridge on which this gulch terminates, at a height of 9000 feet, we saw at last Estes Park, lying 1500 feet below in the glory of the setting sun, an irregular basin, lighted up by the bright waters of the rushing Thompson, guarded by sentinel mountains of fantastic shape and monstrous size, with Long's Peak rising above them all in unapproachable grandeur, while the Snowy Range, with its outlying spurs heavily timbered, come down upon the Park slashed by stupendous canyons lying deep in purple gloom. The rushing river was blood-red, Long's Peak was aflame, the glory of the glowing heaven was given back from earth. Never, nowhere, have I seen anything to equal the view into Estes Park. The mountains "of the land which is very far off" are very near now, but the near is more glorious than the far, and reality than dreamland. The mountain fever seized me, and, giving my tireless horse one encouraging word, he dashed at full gallop over a mile of smooth sward at delirious speed. But I was hungry, and the air was frosty, and I was wondering what the prospects of food and shelter were in this enchanted region, when we came suddenly upon a small lake, close to which was a very trim-looking log cabin, with a flat mud roof, with four smaller ones; picturesquely dotted about near it, two *corrals*,[1]

---

[1] A *corral* is a fenced enclosure for cattle. This word, with *bronco, ranch*, and a few others, are adaptations from the Spanish,

a long shed, in front of which a steer was being killed, a log-dairy with a water-wheel, some hay-piles, and various evidences of comfort; and two men, on serviceable horses, were just bringing in some tolerable cows to be milked. A short, pleasant-looking man ran up to me and shook hands gleefully. which surprised me; but he has since told me that in the evening light he thought I was "Mountain Jim, dressed up as a woman!" I recognised in him a countryman, and he introduced himself as Griffith Evans, a Welshman from the slate quarries near Llanberis. When the cabin-door was opened I saw a good-sized log room, unchinked, however, with windows of infamous glass, looking two ways; a rough stone fireplace, in which pine logs, half as large as I am, were burning; a boarded floor, a round table, two rocking-chairs, a carpet-covered backwoods couch; and skins, Indian bows and arrows, wampum belts, and antlers, fitly decorated the rough walls, and equally fitly rifles were stuck up in the corners. Seven men, smoking, were lying about on the floor, a sick man lay on the couch, and a middle-aged lady sat at the table writing. I went out again and asked Evans if he could take me in, expecting nothing better than a shakedown; but, to my joy, he told me he could give me a cabin to myself, two minutes'

and are used as extensively throughout California and the Territories as is the Spanish or Mexican saddle.

LETTER VII.

"Personality" of Long's Peak—"Mountain Jim"—Lake of the Lilies
—A silent Forest—The Camping Ground—"Ring"—A Lady's
Bower—Dawn and Sunrise—A glorious View—Links of Diamonds—The Ascent of the Peak—The Dog's Lift—Suffering
from Thirst—The Descent—The Bivouac.

ESTES PARK, COLORADO, *October.*

As this account of the ascent of Long's Peak could
not be written at the time, I am much disinclined
to write it, especially as no sort of description within
my powers could enable another to realise the
glorious sublimity, the majestic solitude, and the
unspeakable awfulness and fascination of the scenes
in which I spent Monday, Tuesday, and Wed-
nesday.

Long's Peak, 14,700 feet high, blocks up one end
of Estes Park, and dwarfs all the surrounding mountains. From it on this side rise, snow-born, the
bright St. Vrain, and the Big and Little Thompson.
By sunlight or moonlight its splintered grey crest is
the one object which, in spite of wapiti and bighorn,
skunk and grizzly, unfailingly arrests the eye. From
it come all storms of snow and wind, and the forked
lightnings play round its head like a glory. It is

one of the noblest of mountains, but in one's imagination it grows to be much more than a mountain. It becomes invested with a personality. In its caverns and abysses one comes to fancy that it generates and chains the strong winds, to let them loose in its fury. The thunder becomes its voice, and the lightnings do it homage. Other summits blush under the morning kiss of the sun, and turn pale the next moment; but it detains the first sunlight and holds it round its head for an hour at least, till it pleases to change from rosy red to deep blue; and the sunset, as if spell-bound, lingers latest on its crest. The soft winds which hardly rustle the pine needles down here are raging rudely up there round its motionless summit. The mark of fire is upon it; and though it has passed into a grim repose, it tells of fire and up-heaval as truly, though not as eloquently, as the living volcanoes of Hawaii. Here under its shadow one learns how naturally nature worship, and the propitiation of the forces of nature arose in minds which had no better light.

Long's Peak, "the American Matterhorn," as some call it, was ascended five years ago for the first time. I thought I should like to attempt it, but up to Monday, when Evans left for Denver, cold water was thrown upon the project. It was too late in the season, the winds were likely to be strong, etc.; but just before leaving, Evans said that the weather was looking more settled, and if I did not get farther than the timber line it would be worth going. Soon after he left, "Mountain Jim" came in, and said he would go up as guide, and the two youths who rode here with me from Longmount and I caught at the proposal. Mrs. Edwards at once baked bread for three days, steaks were cut from the steer which hangs up conveniently, and tea, sugar, and butter were benevolently added. Our picnic was not to be a luxurious or "well-found" one, for, in order to avoid the expense of a pack mule, we limited our luggage to what our saddle horses could carry. Behind my saddle I carried three pair of camping blankets and a quilt, which reached to my shoulders. My own boots were so much worn that it was painful to walk, even about the park, in them, so Evans had lent me a pair of his hunting boots, which hung to the horn of my saddle. The horses of the two young men were equally loaded, for we had to prepare for many degrees of frost. " Jim " was a shocking figure ; he had on an old pair of high boots, with a baggy pair of old trousers made of deer hide, held on by an old scarf tucked into them ; a leather shirt, with three or four ragged unbuttoned waist-coats over it ; an old smashed wideawake, from under which his tawny, neglected ringlets hung ; and with his one eye, his one long spur, his knife in his belt, his revolver in his waistcoat pocket, his saddle covered with an old beaver-skin, from which the paws hung

aspen flaunting in red and gold to intensify the blue gloom of the pines, the trickle and murmur of streams fringed with icicles, the strange *sough* of gusts moving among the pine tops—sights and sounds not of the lower earth, but of the solitary, beast-haunted, frozen upper altitudes. From the dry, buff grass of Estes Park we turned off up a trail on the side of a pine-hung gorge, up a steep pine-clothed hill, down to a small valley, rich in fine, sun-cured hay about eighteen inches high, and enclosed by high mountains whose deepest hollow contains a lily-covered lake, fitly named "The Lake of the Lilies." Ah, how magical its beauty was, as it slept in silence, while *there* the dark pines were mirrored motionless in its pale gold, and *here* the great white lily cups and dark green leaves rested on amethyst-coloured water !

From this we ascended into the purple gloom of great pine forests which clothe the skirts of the mountains up to a height of about 11,000 feet, and from their chill and solitary depths we had glimpses of golden atmosphere and rose-lit summits, not of " the land very far off," but of the land nearer now in all its grandeur, gaining in sublimity by nearness— glimpses, too, through a broken vista of purple gorges, of the illimitable Plains lying idealised in the late sunlight, their baked, brown expanse transfigured into the likeness of a sunset sea rolling infinitely in waves of misty gold.

We rode upwards through the gloom on a steep trail blazed through the forest, all my intellect concentrated on avoiding being dragged off my horse by impending branches, or having the blankets badly torn, as those of my companions were, by sharp dead limbs, between which there was hardly room to pass —the horses breathless, and requiring to stop every few yards, though their riders, except myself, were afoot. The gloom of the dense, ancient, silent forest is to me awe-inspiring. On such an evening it is soundless, except for the branches creaking in the soft wind, the frequent snap of decayed timber, and a murmur in the pine tops as of a not distant waterfall, all tending to produce *eeriness* and a sadness " hardly akin to pain." There no lumberer's axe has ever rung. The trees die when they have attained their prime, and stand there, dead and bare, till the fierce mountain winds lay them prostrate. The pines grew smaller and more sparse as we ascended, and the last stragglers wore a tortured, warring look. The timber line was passed, but yet a little higher a slope of mountain meadow dipped to the south-west towards a bright stream trickling under ice and icicles, and there a grove of the beautiful silver spruce marked our camping ground. The trees were in miniature, but so exquisitely arranged that one might well ask what artist's hand had planted them, scattering them here, clumping them there, and training their slim spires towards heaven. Hereafter, when I call up memories of the glorious, the view from this camping ground will come up. Looking east, gorges opened to the distant Plains, then fading into purple grey. Mountains with pine-clothed skirts rose in ranges, or, solitary, uplifted their grey summits, while close behind, but nearly 3000 feet above us, towered the bald white crest of Long's Peak, its huge precipices red with the light of a sun long lost to our eyes. Close to us, in the caverned side of the Peak, was snow that, owing to its position, is eternal. Soon the afterglow came on, and before it faded a big half-moon hung out of the heavens, shining through the silver blue foliage of the pines on the frigid background of snow, and turning the whole into fairyland. The "photo" which accompanies this letter is by a courageous Denver artist who attempted the ascent just before I arrived, but, after camping out at the timber line for a week, was foiled by the perpetual storms, and was driven down again, leaving some very valuable apparatus about 3000 feet from the summit.

Unsaddling and picketing the horses securely, making the beds of pine shoots, and dragging up logs for fuel, warmed us all. " Jim " built up a great fire, and before long we were all sitting round it at supper. It didn't matter much that we had to drink our tea out of the battered meat-tins in which it was boiled, and eat strips of beef reeking with pine smoke without plates or forks.

"Treat Jim as a gentleman and you'll find him one," I had been told; and though his manner was certainly bolder and freer than that of gentlemen generally, no imaginary fault could be found. He was very agreeable as a man of culture as well as a child of nature; the desperado was altogether out of sight. He was very courteous and even kind to me, which was fortunate, as the young men had little idea of showing even ordinary civilities. That night I made the acquaintance of his dog "Ring," said to be the best hunting-dog in Colorado, with the body and legs of a collie, but a head approaching that of a mastiff, a noble face with a wistful human expression, and the most truthful eyes I ever saw in an animal. His master loves him if he loves anything, but in his savage moods ill-treats him. "Ring's" devotion never swerves, and his truthful eyes are rarely taken off his master's face. He is almost human in his intelligence, and, unless he is told to do so, he never takes notice of any one but "Jim." In a tone as if speaking to a human being, his master, pointing to me, said, "Ring, go to that lady, and don't leave her again to-night." "Ring" at once came to me, looked into my face, laid his head on my shoulder, and then lay down beside me with his head on my lap, but never taking his eyes from "Jim's" face.

The long shadows of the pines lay upon the frosted grass, an aurora leaped fitfully, and the moonlight, though intensely bright, was pale beside the red, leaping flames of our pine logs and their red glow on our gear, ourselves, and Ring's truthful face. One of the young men sang a Latin student's song and two negro melodies ; the other, " Sweet Spirit, hear my Prayer."   " Jim " sang one of Moore's melodies in a singular falsetto, and all together sang " The Star-spangled Banner" and " The Red, White, and Blue."   Then " Jim " recited a very clever poem of his own composition, and told some fearful Indian stories.   A group of small silver spruces away from the fire was my sleeping-place.   The artist who had been up there had so woven and interlaced their lower branches as to form a bower, affording at once shelter from the wind and a most agreeable privacy.   It was thickly strewn with young pine shoots, and these, when covered with a blanket, with an inverted saddle for a pillow, made a luxurious bed.   The mercury at 9 P.M. was 12° below the freezing point.   " Jim," after a last look at the horses, made a huge fire, and stretched himself out beside it, but " Ring " lay at my back to keep me warm.   I could not sleep, but the night passed rapidly.   I was anxious about the ascent, for gusts of ominous sound swept through the pines at intervals.   Then wild animals howled, and " Ring" was perturbed in spirit about them.   Then it was strange to see the notorious desperado, a red-handed man, sleeping as quietly as innocence sleeps. But, above all, it was exciting to lie there, with no better shelter than a bower of pines, on a mountain 11,000 feet high, in the very heart of the Rocky Range, under twelve degrees of frost, hearing sounds of wolves, with shivering stars looking through the fragrant canopy, with arrowy pines for bed-posts, and for a night lamp the red flames of a camp fire.

Day dawned long before the sun rose, pure and lemon-coloured. The rest were looking after the horses, when one of the students came running to tell me that I must come farther down the slope, for " Jim " said he had never seen such a sunrise. From the chill, grey Peak above, from the everlasting snows, from the silvered pines, down through mountain ranges with their depths of Tyrian purple, we looked to where the Plains lay cold, in blue grey, like a morning sea against a far horizon. Suddenly, as a dazzling streak at first, but enlarging rapidly into a dazzling sphere, the sun wheeled above the grey line, a light and glory as when it was first created. " Jim" involuntarily and reverently uncovered his head, and exclaimed, " I believe there is a God!" I felt as if, Parsee-like, I must worship. The grey of the Plains changed to purple, the sky was all one rose-red flush, on which vermilion cloud-streaks rested; the ghastly peaks gleamed like rubies, the earth and heavens were new-created. Surely " the

Most High dwelleth not in temples made with hands !" For a full hour those Plains simulated the ocean, down to whose limitless expanse of purple, cliffs, rocks, and promontories swept down.

By seven we had finished breakfast, and passed into the ghastlier solitudes above, I riding as far as what, rightly or wrongly, are called the "Lava Beds," an expanse of large and small boulders, with snow in their crevices. It was very cold; some water which we crossed was frozen hard enough to bear the horse. "Jim" had advised me against taking any wraps, and my thin Hawaiian riding-dress, only fit for the tropics, was penetrated by the keen air. The rarefied atmosphere soon began to oppress our breathing, and I found that Evans's boots were so large that I had no foothold. Fortunately, before the real difficulty of the ascent began, we found, under a rock, a pair of small over-shoes, probably left by the Hayden exploring expedition, which just lasted for the day. As we were leaping from rock to rock, "Jim" said, "I was thinking in the night about your travelling alone, and wondering where you carried your Derringer, for I could see no signs of it." On my telling him that I travelled unarmed, he could hardly believe it, and adjured me to get a revolver at once.

On arriving at the "Notch" (a literal gate of rock), we found ourselves absolutely on the knife-like ridge or backbone of Long's Peak, only a few feet wide, covered with colossal boulders and fragments, and on the other side shelving in one precipitous, snow-patched sweep of 3000 feet to a picturesque hollow, containing a lake of pure green water. Other lakes, hidden among dense pine woods, were farther off, while close above us rose the Peak, which, for about 500 feet, is a smooth, gaunt, inaccessible-looking pile of granite. Passing through the " Notch," we looked along the nearly inaccessible side of the Peak, composed of boulders and *débris* of all shapes and sizes, through which appeared broad, smooth ribs of reddish-coloured granite, looking as if they upheld the towering rock-mass above. I usually dislike bird's-eye and panoramic views, but, though from a mountain, this was not one. Serrated ridges, not much lower than that on which we stood, rose, one beyond another, far as that pure atmosphere could carry the vision, broken into awful chasms deep with ice and snow, rising into pinnacles piercing the heavenly blue with their cold, barren grey, on, on for ever, till the most distant range upbore unsullied snow alone. There were fair lakes mirroring the dark pine woods, canyons dark and blue-black with unbroken expanses of pines, snow-slashed pinnacles, wintry heights frowning upon lovely parks, watered and wooded, lying in the lap of summer; North Park floating off into the blue distance, Middle Park closed till another season, the sunny slopes of Estes Park, and winding down among the mountains the snowy

terror. I was roped to " Jim," but it was of no use,
my feet were paralysed and slipped on the bare rock,
and he said it was useless to try to go that way, and we
retraced our steps. I wanted to return to the " Notch,"
knowing that my incompetence would detain the
party, and one of the young men said almost plainly
that a woman was a dangerous encumbrance, but the
trapper replied shortly that if it were not to take a lady
up he would not go up at all. He went on to explore,
and reported that further progress on the correct line
of ascent was blocked by ice; and then for two hours
we descended, lowering ourselves by our hands from
rock to rock along a boulder-strewn sweep of 4000
feet, patched with ice and snow, and perilous from
rolling stones. My fatigue, giddiness, and pain from
bruised ankles, and arms half pulled out of their
sockets, were so great that I should never have gone
half-way had not " Jim," *nolens volens*, dragged me
along with a patience and skill, and withal a deter-
mination that I should ascend the Peak, which never
failed. After descending about 2000 feet to avoid
the ice, we got into a deep ravine with inaccessible
sides, partly filled with ice and snow and partly with
large and small fragments of rock, which were constantly giving way, rendering the footing very insecure. That part to me was two hours of painful and
unwilling submission to the inevitable; of trembling,
slipping, straining, of smooth ice appearing when it

was least expected, and of weak entreaties to be left behind while the others went on. " Jim " always said that there was no danger, that there was only a short bad bit ahead, and that I should go up even if he carried me !

Slipping, faltering, gasping from the exhausting toil in the rarefied air, with throbbing hearts and panting lungs, we reached the top of the gorge and squeezed ourselves between two gigantic fragments of rock by a passage called the " Dog's Lift," when I climbed on the shoulders of one man and then was hauled up. This introduced us by an abrupt turn round the south-west angle of the Peak to a narrow shelf of considerable length, rugged, uneven, and so overhung by the cliff in some places that it is neces- sary to crouch to pass at all. Above, the Peak looks nearly vertical for 400 feet; and below, the most tremendous precipice I have ever seen descends in one unbroken fall. This is usually considered the most dangerous part of the ascent, but it does not seem so to me, for such foothold as there is is secure, and one fancies that it is possible to hold on with the hands. But there, and on the final, and, to my thinking, the worst part of the climb, one slip, and a breathing, thinking, human being would lie 3000 feet below, a shapeless, bloody heap! "Ring" refused to traverse the Ledge, and remained at the " Lift " howling piteously.

From thence the view is more magnificent even

than that from the "Notch." At the foot of the
precipice below us lay a lovely lake, wood embo-
somed, from or near which the bright St. Vrain and
other streams take their rise. I thought how their
clear cold waters, growing turbid in the affluent
flats, would heat under the tropic sun, and eventually
form part of that great ocean river which renders
our far-off islands habitable by impinging on their
shores. Snowy ranges, one behind the other, extended to the distant horizon, folding in their wintry
embrace the beauties of Middle Park. Pike's Peak,
more than one hundred miles off, lifted that vast but
shapeless summit which is the landmark of Southern
Colorado. There were snow patches, snow slashes,
snow abysses, snow forlorn and soiled-looking, snow
pure and dazzling, snow glistening above the purple
robe of pine worn by all the mountains ; while away
to the east, in limitless breadth, stretched the green-
grey of the endless Plains. Giants everywhere reared
their splintered crests. From thence, with a single
sweep, the eye takes in a distance of 300 miles—
that distance to the west, north, and south being
made up of mountains ten, eleven, twelve, and thirteen
thousand feet in height, dominated by Long's Peak,
Gray's Peak, and Pike's Peak, all nearly the height
of Mont Blanc ! On the Plains we traced the rivers
by their fringe of cotton-woods to the distant Platte,
and between us and them lay glories of mountain,

canyon, and lake, sleeping in depths of blue and purple most ravishing to the eye.

As we crept from the lodge round a horn of rock, I beheld what made me perfectly sick and dizzy to look at—the terminal Peak itself—a smooth, cracked face or wall of pink granite, as nearly perpendicular as anything could well be up which it was possible to climb, well deserving the name of the "American Matterhorn." [1]

Scaling, not climbing, is the correct term for this last ascent. It took one hour to accomplish 500 feet, pausing for breath every minute or two. The only foothold was in narrow cracks or on minute projections on the granite. To get a toe in these cracks, or here and there on a scarcely obvious projection, while crawling on hands and knees, all the while tortured with thirst and gasping and struggling for breath, this was the climb; but at last the Peak was won. A grand, well-defined mountain-top it is, a nearly level acre of boulders, with precipitous sides all round, the one we came up being the only accessible one.

It was not possible to remain long. One of the young men was seriously alarmed by bleeding from

[1] Let no practical mountaineer be allured by my description into the ascent of Long's Peak. Truly terrible as it was to me, to a member of the Alpine Club it would not be a feat worth performing.

the lungs, and the intense dryness of the day and the rarefaction of the air, at a height of nearly 15,000 feet, made respiration very painful. There is always water on the Peak, but it was frozen as hard as a rock, and the sucking of ice and snow increases thirst. We all suffered severely from the want of water, and the gasping for breath made our mouths and tongues so dry that articulation was difficult, and the speech of all unnatural.

From the summit were seen in unrivalled combination all the views which had rejoiced our eyes during the ascent. It was something at last to stand upon the storm-rent crown of this lonely sentinel of the Rocky Range, on one of the mightiest of the vertebræ of the backbone of the North American continent, and to see the waters start for both oceans. Uplifted above love and hate and storms of passion, calm amidst the eternal silences, fanned by zephyrs and bathed in living blue, peace rested for that one bright day on the Peak, as if it were some region

> "Where falls not rain, or hail, or any snow,
> Or ever wind blows loudly."

We placed our names, with the date of ascent, in a tin within a crevice, and descended to the Ledge, sitting on the smooth granite, getting our feet into cracks and against projections, and letting ourselves down by our hands, "Jim" going before me, so that I might steady my feet against his powerful shoulders. I was no longer giddy, and faced the precipice of 3500 feet without a shiver. Repassing the Ledge and Lift, we accomplished the descent through 1500 feet of ice and snow, with many falls and bruises, but no worse mishap, and there separated, the young men taking the steepest but most direct way to the Notch, with the intention of getting ready for the march home, and "Jim" and I taking what he thought the safer route for me — a descent over boulders for 2000 feet, and then a tremendous ascent to the "Notch." I had various falls, and once hung by my frock, which caught on a rock, and "Jim" severed it with his hunting-knife, upon which I fell into a crevice full of soft snow. We were driven lower down the mountains than he had intended by impassable tracts of ice, and the ascent was tremendous. For the last 200 feet the boulders were of enormous size, and the steepness fearful. Sometimes I drew myself up on hands and knees, sometimes crawled; sometimes "Jim" pulled me up by my arms or a lariat, and sometimes I stood on his shoulders, or he made steps for me of his feet and hands, but at six we stood on the Notch in the splendour of the sinking sun, all colour deepening, all peaks glorifying, all shadows purpling, all peril past.

"Jim" had parted with his *brusquerie* when we parted from the students, and was gentle and considerate beyond anything, though I knew that he must be grievously disappointed, both in my courage and strength. Water was an object of earnest desire. My tongue rattled in my mouth, and I could hardly articulate. It is good for one's sympathies to have for once a severe experience of thirst. Truly, there was

> " Water, water, everywhere,
>   But not a drop to drink."

Three times its apparent gleam deceived even the mountaineer's practised eye, but we found only a foot of " glare ice." At last, in a deep hole, he succeeded in breaking the ice, and by putting one's arm far down one could scoop up a little water in one's hand, but it was tormentingly insufficient. With great difficulty and much assistance I recrossed the " Lava Beds," was carried to the horse and lifted upon him, and when we reached the camping ground I was lifted off him, and laid on the ground wrapped up in blankets, a humiliating termination of a great exploit. The horses were saddled, and the young men were all ready to start, but "Jim" quietly said, " Now, gentlemen, I want a good night's rest, and we shan't stir from here to-night." I believe they were really glad to have it so, as one of them was quite "finished." I retired to my arbour, wrapped myself in a roll of blankets, and was soon asleep. When I woke, the moon was high shining through the silvery branches, whitening the bald Peak above, and glittering on the great abyss of snow behind, and pine logs were blazing like a bonfire in the cold still air. My feet were so icy cold that I could not sleep again, and getting some blankets to sit in, and making a roll of them for my back, I sat for two hours by the camp fire. It was weird and gloriously beautiful. The students were asleep not far off in their blankets with their feet towards the fire. "Ring" lay on one side of me with his fine head on my arm, and his master sat smoking, with the fire lighting up the handsome side of his face, and except for the tones of our voices, and an occasional crackle and splutter as a pine knot blazed up, there was no sound on the mountain side. The beloved stars of my far-off home were overhead, the Plough and Pole Star, with their steady light; the glittering Pleiades, looking larger than I ever saw them, and "Orion's studded belt" shining gloriously. Once only some wild animals prowled near the camp, when "Ring," with one bound, disappeared from my side; and the horses, which were picketed by the stream, broke their lariats, stampeded, and came rushing wildly towards the fire, and it was fully half an hour before they were caught and quiet was restored. "Jim," or Mr. Nugent, as I always scrupulously called him, told stories of his early youth, and of a great sorrow which had led him to embark on a lawless and desperate life. His

LETTER VIII.

ESTES PARK, COLORADO TERRITORY, *October 2.*

How time has slipped by I do not know. This is a glorious region, and the air and life are intoxicating. I live mainly out of doors and on horseback, wear my half threadbare Hawaiian dress, sleep sometimes under the stars on a bed of pine boughs, ride on a Mexican saddle, and hear once more the low music of my Mexican spurs. "There's a stranger! Heave arf a brick at him!" is said by many travellers to express the feeling of the new settlers in these Territories. This is not my experience in my cheery mountain home. How the rafters ring as I write with songs and mirth, while the pitch-pine logs blaze and crackle in the chimney, and the fine snow-dust drives in through the chinks and forms mimic snow-wreaths on the floor, and the wind raves and howls and plays among the creaking pine branches and snaps them short off, and the lightning plays round the blasted top of Long's Peak, and the hardy hunters divert themselves with the thought that when I go to bed I must turn out and face the storm!

You will ask, "What is Estes Park?" This name, with the quiet Midland Counties' sound, suggests "park palings" well lichened, a lodge with a curtseying woman, fallow-deer, and a Queen Anne mansion. Such as it is, Estes Park is mine. It is unsurveyed, "no man's land," and mine by right of love, appropriation, and appreciation; by the seizure of its peerless sunrises and sunsets, its glorious afterglow, its blazing noons, its hurricanes sharp and furious, its wild auroras, its glories of mountain and forest, of canyon, lake, and river, and the stereotyping them all in my memory. Mine, too, in a better than the sportsman's sense, are its majestic wapiti, which play and fight under the pines in the early morning, as securely as fallow-deer under our English oaks; its graceful "black-tails," swift of foot; its superb big-horns, whose noble leader is to be seen now and then with his classic head against the blue sky on the top of a colossal rock; its sneaking mountain lion with his hideous nocturnal caterwaulings, the great "grizzly," the beautiful skunk, the wary beaver, who is always making lakes, damming and turning streams, cutting down young cotton-woods, and setting an example of thrift and industry; the wolf, greedy and cowardly; the coyote and the lynx, and all the lesser fry of mink, marten, cat, hare, fox, squirrel, and chipmonk, as well as things that fly, from the eagle down to the crested blue-jay. May their number never be less, in spite of the hunter who kills for food and gain, and the sportsman who kills and marauds for pastime!

But still I have not answered the natural question,[1] "What is Estes Park?" Among the striking peculiarities of these mountains are hundreds of high-lying valleys, large and small, at heights varying from 6000 to 11,000 feet. The most important are North Park, held by hostile Indians; Middle Park, famous for hot springs and trout; South Park, rich in minerals; and San Luis Park. South Park is 10,000 feet high, a great rolling prairie 70 miles long, well grassed and watered, but nearly closed by snow in winter. But Parks innumerable are scattered throughout the mountains, most of them unnamed, and others nicknamed by the hunters or trappers who have made them their temporary resorts. They always lie far within the flaming Foot Hills, their exquisite stretches of flowery pastures dotted artistically with clumps of trees sloping lawnlike to bright swift streams full of red-

---

[1] Nor should I at this time, had not Henry Kingsley, Lord Dunraven, and "The Field," divulged the charms and whereabouts of these "happy hunting grounds," with the certain result of directing a stream of tourists into the solitary, beast-haunted paradise.

waistcoated trout, or running up in soft glades into
the dark forest, above which the snow-peaks rise in
their infinite majesty. Some are bits of meadow a
mile long and very narrow, with a small stream, a
beaver-dam, and a pond made by beaver industry.
Hundreds of these can only be reached by riding in
the bed of a stream, or by scrambling up some narrow
canyon till it debouches on the fairy-like stretch
above. These parks are the feeding-grounds of innumerable wild animals, and some, like one three
miles off, seem chosen for the process of antler-cast-
ing, the grass being covered for at least a square mile
with the magnificent branching horns of the elk.

Estes Park combines the beauties of all. Dismiss
all thoughts of the Midland Counties. For park
palings there are mountains, forest skirted, 9000,
11,000, 14,000 feet high; for a lodge, two sentinel
peaks of granite guarding the only feasible entrance;
and for a Queen Anne mansion an unchinked log
cabin with a vault of sunny blue overhead. The
park is most irregularly shaped, and contains hardly
any level grass. It is an aggregate of lawns, slopes,
and glades, about eighteen miles in length, but never
more than two miles in width. The Big Thompson,
a bright, rapid trout-stream, snow-born on Long's Peak
a few miles higher, takes all sorts of magical twists,
vanishing and reappearing unexpectedly, glancing
among lawns, rushing through romantic ravines,

ESTES PARK.

BAD FOOTING FOR HORSES.

"GRAND CRATER."   *From a Photo.*

"LAVA BEDS," LONG'S PEAK. *From a Photo.*

MY HOME IN THE ROCKY MOUNTAINS.

From a Sketch.

THE GREAT DIVIDE.

From a Photo.

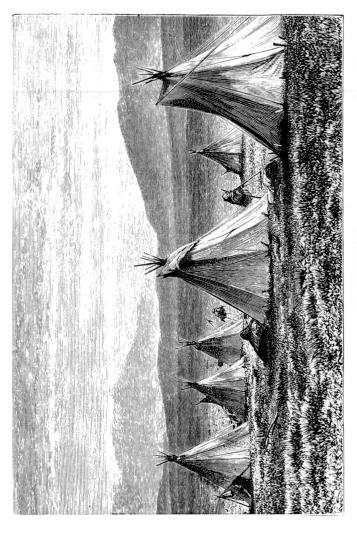

AN INDIAN CAMP.

From a Photo.

everywhere making music through the still, long nights. Here and there the lawns are so smooth, the trees so artistically grouped, a lake makes such an artistic foreground, or a waterfall comes tumbling down with such an apparent feeling for the picturesque, that I am almost angry with Nature for her close imitation of art. But in another hundred yards Nature, glorious, unapproachable, inimitable, is herself again, raising one's thoughts reverently upwards to her Creator and ours. Grandeur and sublimity, not softness, are the features of Estes Park. The glades which begin so softly are soon lost in the dark primæval forests, with their peaks of rosy granite, and their stretches of granite blocks piled and poised by nature in some mood of fury. The streams are lost in canyons nearly or quite inaccessible, awful in their blackness and darkness; every valley ends in mystery; seven mountain ranges raise their frowning barriers between us and the Plains, and at the south end of the park Long's Peak rises to a height of 14,700 feet, with his bare, scathed head slashed with eternal snow. The lowest part of the Park is 7500 feet high; and though the sun is hot during the day, the mercury hovers near the freezing-point every night of the summer. An immense quantity of snow falls, but partly owing to the tremendous winds which drift it into the deep valleys, and partly to the bright warm sun of the winter months, the Park is never

snowed up, and a number of cattle and horses are
wintered out of doors on its sun-cured, saccharine
grasses, of which the *gramma* grass is the most valuable. The soil here, as elsewhere in the neighbourhood, is nearly everywhere coarse, grey, granitic dust,
produced probably by the disintegration of the surrounding mountains. It does not hold water, and is
never wet in any weather. There are no thaws here.
The snow mysteriously disappears by rapid evaporation. Oats grow, but do not ripen, and, when well
advanced, are cut and stacked for winter fodder.
Potatoes yield abundantly, and, though not very large,
are of the best quality, mealy throughout. Evans
has not attempted anything else, and probably the
more succulent vegetables would require irrigation.
The wild flowers are gorgeous and innumerable,
though their beauty, which culminates in July and
August, was over before I arrived, and the recent
snow-flurries have finished them. The time between
winter and winter is very short, and the flowery
growth and blossom of a whole year are compressed
into two months. Here are dandelions, buttercups,
larkspurs, harebells, violets, roses, blue gentian, colum-
bine, painter's brush, and fifty others, blue and yellow
predominating; and though their blossoms are stiffened
by the cold every morning, they are starring the grass
and drooping over the brook long before noon, making the most of their brief lives in the sunshine. Of

ferns, after many a long hunt, I have only found the
Cystopteris fragilis and the *Blechnum spicant*, but I
hear that the *Pteris aquilina* is also found. Snakes
and mosquitoes do not appear to be known here.
Coming almost direct from the tropics, one is dis-
satisfied with the uniformity of the foliage; indeed,
foliage can hardly be written of, as the trees properly
so called at this height are exclusively *Coniferæ*, and
bear needles instead of leaves. In places there are
patches of spindly aspens, which have turned a lemon-
yellow, and along the streams bear-cherries, vines,
and roses lighten the gulches with their variegated
crimson leaves. The pines are not imposing, either
from their girth or height. Their colouring is blackish-
green, and though they are effective singly or in groups,
they are sombre and almost funereal when densely
massed, as here, along the mountain sides. The timber line is at a height of about 11,000 feet, and is
singularly well defined. The most attractive tree I
have seen is the silver spruce, *Abies Englemanii*, near
of kin to what is often called the balsam-fir. Its
shape and colour are both beautiful. My heart
warms towards it, and I frequent all the places where
I can find it. It looks as if a soft, blue, silver powder
had fallen on its deep-green needles, or as if a bluish
hoar-frost, which must melt at noon, were resting
upon it. Anyhow, one can hardly believe that the
beauty is permanent, and survives the summer heat

and the winter cold. The universal tree here is the *Pinus ponderosa*, but it never attains any very considerable size, and there is nothing to compare with the red-woods of the Sierra Nevada, far less with the sequoias of California.

As I have written before, Estes Park is twenty-five and a half miles from Longmount, the nearest settlement, and it can be reached on horseback only by the steep and devious track by which I came, passing through a narrow rift in the top of a precipitous ridge, 9000 feet high, called the Devil's Gate. Evans takes a lumber waggon with four horses over the mountains, and a Colorado engineer would have no difficulty in making a waggon road. In several of the gulches over which the track hangs there are the remains of waggons which have come to grief in the attempt to emulate Evans's feat, which, without evidence, I should have supposed to be impossible. It is an awful road. The only settlers in the Park are Griffith Evans, and a married man a mile higher up. "Mountain Jim's" cabin is in the entrance gulch, four miles off, and there is not another cabin for eighteen miles towards the Plains. The Park is unsurveyed, and the huge tract of mountainous country beyond is almost altogether unexplored. Elk-hunters occasionally come up and camp out here; but the two settlers, who, however, are only squatters, for various reasons are not disposed to encourage such visitors. When

Evans, who is a very successful hunter, came here, he came on foot, and for some time after settling here he carried the flour and necessaries required by his family on his back over the mountains.

As I intend to make Estes Park my headquarters until the winter sets in, I must make you acquainted with my surroundings and mode of living. The "Queen Anne Mansion" is represented by a log cabin made of big hewn logs. The chinks should be filled with mud and lime, but these are wanting. The roof is formed of barked young spruce, then a layer of hay, and an outer coating of mud, all nearly flat. The floors are roughly boarded. The "living-room" is about sixteen feet square, and has a rough stone chimney in which pine logs are always burning. At one end there is a door into a small bedroom, and at the other a door into a small eating-room, at the table of which we feed in relays. This opens into a very small kitchen with a great American cooking-stove, and there are two "bed-closets" besides. Although rude, it is comfortable, except for the draughts. The fine snow drives in through the chinks and covers the floors, but sweeping it out at intervals is both fun and exercise. There are no heaps or rubbish-places outside. Near it, on the slope under the pines, is a pretty two-roomed cabin, and beyond that, near the lake, is my cabin, a very rough one. My door opens into a little room with a stone chimney, and that again into a small room with a hay bed, a chair with a tin basin on it, a shelf and some pegs. A small window looks on the lake, and the glories of the sunrises which I see from it are indescribable. Neither of my doors has a lock, and, to say the truth, neither will shut, as the wood has swelled. Below the house, on the stream which issues from the lake, there is a beautiful log dairy, with a water-wheel outside, used for churning. Besides this, there are a *corral*, a shed for the waggon, a room for the hired man, and shelters for horses and weakly calves. All these things are necessaries at this height.

The ranchmen are two Welshmen, Evans and Edwards, each with a wife and family. The men are as diverse as they can be. "Griff," as Evans is called, is short and small, and is hospitable, careless, reckless, jolly, social, convivial, peppery, good-natured, "nobody's enemy but his own." He had the wit and taste to find out Estes Park, where people have found him out, and have induced him to give them food and lodging, and add cabin to cabin to take them in. He is a splendid shot, an expert and successful hunter, a bold mountaineer, a good rider, a capital cook, and a generally "jolly fellow." His cheery laugh rings through the cabin from the early morning, and is contagious, and when the rafters ring at night with such songs as "D'ye ken John Peel?" "Auld Lang Syne," and "John Brown," what would the chorus be

without poor " Griff's " voice? What would Estes
Park be without him, indeed? When he went to
Denver lately, we missed him as we should have
missed the sunshine, and perhaps more. In the early
morning, when Long's Peak is red, and the grass
crackles with the hoar-frost, he arouses me with a
cheery thump on my door. "We're going cattle-
hunting, will you come?" or, "Will you help to drive
in the cattle? you can take your pick of the horses.
I want another hand." Free-hearted, lavish, popular,
poor " Griff" loves liquor too well for his prosperity,
and is always tormented by debt. He makes lots of
money, but puts it into "a bag with holes." He has
fifty horses and 1000 head of cattle, many of which
are his own, wintering up here, and makes no end of
money by taking in people at eight dollars a week,
yet it all goes somehow. He has a most industrious
wife, a girl of seventeen, and four younger children,
all musical, but the wife has to work like a slave;
and though he is a kind husband, her lot, as compared
with her lord's, is like that of a squaw. Edwards,
his partner, is his exact opposite, tall, thin, and
condemnatory - looking, keen, industrious, saving,
grave, a teetotaller, grieved for all reasons at Evans's
follies, and rather grudging; as naturally unpopular
as Evans is popular; a " decent man," who, with his
industrious wife, will certainly make money as fast
as Evans loses it.

I pay eight dollars a week, which includes the unlimited use of a horse, when one can be found and caught. We breakfast at seven on beef, potatoes, tea, coffee, new bread, and butter. Two pitchers of cream and two of milk are replenished as fast as they are exhausted. Dinner at twelve is a repetition of the breakfast, but with the coffee omitted and a gigantic pudding added. Tea at six is a repetition of breakfast. "Eat whenever you are hungry, you can always get milk and bread in the kitchen," Evans says—"eat as much as you can, it'll do you good," and we all eat like hunters. There is no change of food. The steer which was being killed on my arrival is now being eaten through from head to tail, the meat being hacked off quite promiscuously, without any regard to joints. In this dry, rarefied air, the outside of the flesh blackens and hardens, and though the weather may be hot, the carcass keeps sweet for two or three months. The bread is super-excellent, but the poor wives seem to be making and baking it all day.

The regular household living and eating together at this time consists of a very intelligent and high-minded American couple, Mr. and Mrs. Dewy, people whose character, culture, and society I should value anywhere; a young Englishman, brother of a celebrated African traveller, who, because he rides on an English saddle, and clings to some other insular peculiarities, is called "The Earl;" a miner prospecting for silver; a young man, the type of intelligent, practical "Young America," whose health showed consumptive tendencies when he was in business, and who is living a hunter's life here; a grown-up niece of Evans; and a melancholy-looking hired man. A mile off there is an industrious married settler, and four miles off, in the gulch leading to the Park, "Mountain Jim," otherwise Mr. Nugent, is posted. His business as a trapper takes him daily up to the beaver-dams in Black Canyon to look after his traps, and he generally spends some time in or about our cabin, not, I can see, to Evans's satisfaction. For, in truth, this blue hollow, lying solitary at the foot of Long's Peak, is a miniature world of great interest, in which love, jealousy, hatred, envy, pride, unselfishness, greed, selfishness, and self-sacrifice can be studied hourly, and there is always the unpleasantly exciting risk of an open quarrel with the neighbouring desperado, whose "I'll shoot you!" has more than once been heard in the cabin.

The party, however, has often been increased by "campers," either elk hunters or "prospectors" for silver or locations, who feed with us and join us in the evening. They get little help from Evans, either as to elk or locations, and go away disgusted and unsuccessful. Two Englishmen of refinement and culture camped out here prospecting a few weeks ago, and then, contrary to advice, crossed the mountains into North Park, where gold is said to abound, and it is believed that they have fallen victims to the bloodthirsty Indians of that region. Of course, we never get letters or newspapers unless some one rides to Longmount for them. Two or three novels and a copy of *Our New West* are our literature. Our latest newspaper is seventeen days old. Somehow the Park seems to become the natural limit of our interests so far as they appear in conversation at table. The last grand aurora, the prospect of a snow-storm, track and sign of elk and grizzly, rumours of a big-horn herd near the lake, the canyons in which the Texan cattle were last seen, the merits of different rifles, the progress of two obvious love affairs, the probability of some one coming up from the Plains with letters, "Mountain Jim's" latest mood or escapade, and the merits of his dog "Ring" as compared with those of Evans's dog "Plunk," are among the topics which are never abandoned as exhausted.

On Sunday work is nominally laid aside, but most of the men go out hunting or fishing till the evening, when we have the harmonium and much sacred music and singing in parts. To be alone in the Park from the afternoon till the last glory of the afterglow has faded, with no books but a Bible and Prayer-book, is truly delightful. No worthier temple for a "Te Deum" or "Gloria in Excelsis" could be found than this "temple not made with hands," in which one may worship without being distracted by the sight of bonnets of endless form, and curiously intricate " back hair," and countless oddities of changing fashion.

I shall not soon forget my first night here.

Somewhat dazed by the rarefied air, entranced by the glorious beauty, slightly puzzled by the motley company, whose faces loomed not always quite distinctly through the cloud of smoke produced by eleven pipes, I went to my solitary cabin at nine, attended by Evans. It was very dark, and it seemed a long way off. Something howled—Evans said it was a wolf—and owls apparently innumerable hooted incessantly. The pole-star, exactly opposite my cabin door, burned like a lamp. The frost was sharp. Evans opened the door, lighted a candle, and left me, and I was soon in my hay bed. I was frightened—that is, afraid of being frightened, it was so eerie; but sleep soon got the better of my fears. I was awoke by a heavy breathing, a noise something like sawing under the floor, and a pushing and upheaving, all very loud. My candle was all burned, and, in truth, I dared not stir. The noise went on for an hour fully, when, just as I thought the floor had been made sufficiently thin for all purposes of ingress, the sounds abruptly ceased, and I fell asleep again. My hair was not, as it ought to have been, white in the morning!

I was dressed by seven, our breakfast-hour, and

when I reached the great cabin and told my story, Evans laughed hilariously, and Edwards contorted his face dismally. They told me that there was a skunk's lair under my cabin, and that they dare not make any attempt to dislodge him for fear of rendering the cabin untenable. They have tried to trap him since, but without success, and each night the noisy performance is repeated. I think he is sharpening his claws on the under side of my floor, as the grizzlies sharpen theirs upon the trees. The odour with which this creature, truly named Mephitis, can overpower its assailants is truly *awful*. We were driven out of the cabin for some hours merely by the passage of one across the *corral*. The bravest man is a coward in its neighbourhood. Dogs rub their noses on the ground till they bleed when they have touched the fluid, and even die of the vomiting produced by the effluvia. The odour can be smelt a mile off. If clothes are touched by the fluid they must be destroyed. At present its fur is very valuable. Several have been killed since I came. A shot well aimed at the spine secures one safely, and an experienced dog can kill one by leaping upon it suddenly without being exposed to danger. It is a beautiful beast, about the size and length of a fox, with long thick black or dark-brown fur, and two white streaks from the head to the long bushy tail. The claws of its fore-feet are long and polished. Yesterday one was

seen rushing from the dairy and was shot. "Plunk,"
the big dog, touched it, and has to be driven into
exile. The body was valiantly removed by a man
with a long fork, and carried to a running stream, but
we are nearly choked with the odour from the spot
where it fell. I hope that my skunk will enjoy a
quiet spirit so long as we are near neighbours.

October 3.

This is surely one of the most entrancing spots
on earth. Oh, that I could paint with pen or
brush! From my bed I look on Mirror Lake, and
with the very earliest dawn, when objects are not
discernible, it lies there absolutely still, a purplish
lead-colour. Then suddenly into its mirror flash
inverted peaks, at first a bright orange, then changing into red, making the dawn darker all round.
This is a new sight, each morning new. Then the
peaks fade, and when morning is no longer "spread
upon the mountains," the pines are mirrored in my
lake almost as solid objects, and the glory steals
downwards, and a red flush warms the clear atmosphere of the Park, and the hoar-frost sparkles and
the crested blue jays step forth daintily on the jewelled grass. The majesty and beauty grow on me
daily. As I crossed from my cabin just now, and
the long mountain shadows lay on the grass, and
form and colour gained new meanings, I was almost

false to Hawaii; I couldn't go on writing for the
glory of the sunset, but went out and sat on a rock
to see the deepening blue in the dark canyons, and
the peaks becoming rose colour one by one, then
fading into sudden ghastliness, the awe-inspiring
heights of Long's Peak fading last. Then came the
glories of the afterglow, when the orange and lemon
of the east faded into gray, and then gradually the
gray for some distance above the horizon brightened
into a cold blue, and above the blue into a broad band
of rich, warm red, with an upper band of rose colour;
above it hung a big cold moon. This is the "daily
miracle" of evening, as the blazing peaks in the
darkness of Mirror Lake are the miracle of morning.
Perhaps this scenery is not lovable, but, as if it were a
strong stormy character, it has an intense fascination.

The routine of my day is breakfast at seven, then
I go back and "do" my cabin and draw water from
the lake, read a little, loaf a little, return to the big
cabin and sweep it alternately with Mrs. Dewy, after
which she reads aloud till dinner at twelve. Then I
ride with Mr. Dewy, or by myself, or with Mrs.
Dewy, who is learning to ride cavalier fashion in
order to accompany her invalid husband, or go after
cattle till supper at six. After that we all sit in the
living-room, and I settle down to write to you, or
mend my clothes, which are dropping to pieces.
Some sit round the table playing at eucre, the strange

hunters and prospectors lie on the floor smoking, and rifles are cleaned, bullets cast, fishing-flies made, fishing-tackle repaired, boots are waterproofed, part-songs are sung, and about half-past eight I cross the crisp grass to my cabin, always expecting to find something in it. We all wash our own clothes, and as my stock is so small, some part of every day has to be spent at the wash-tub. Politeness and propriety always prevail in our mixed company, and though various grades of society are represented, true democratic equality prevails, not its counterfeit, and there is neither forwardness on one side nor condescension on the other.

Evans left for Denver ten days ago, taking his wife and family to the Plains for the winter, and the mirth of our party departed with him. Edwards is sombre, except when he lies on the floor in the evening, and tells stories of his march through Georgia with Sherman. I gave Evans a 100-dollar note to change, and asked him to buy me a horse for my tour, and for three days we have expected him. The mail depends on him. I have had no letters from you for five weeks, and can hardly curb my impatience. I ride or walk three or four miles out on the Longmount trail two or three times a day to look for him. Others, for different reasons, are nearly equally anxious. After dark we start at every sound, and every time the dogs bark all the able-bodied of us turn out *en masse*. "Wait for the waggon" has become a nearly maddening joke.

October 9.

The letter and newspaper fever has seized on every one. We have sent at last to Longmount. This evening I rode out on the Longmount trail towards dusk, escorted by "Mountain Jim," and in the distance we saw a waggon with four horses and a saddle-horse behind, and the driver waved a handkerchief, the concerted signal if I were the possessor of a horse. We turned back, galloping down the long hill as fast as two good horses could carry us, and gave the joyful news. It was an hour before the waggon arrived, bringing not Evans but two "campers" of suspicious aspect, who have pitched their camp close to my cabin! You cannot imagine what it is to be locked in by these mountain walls, and not to know where your letters are lying. Later on, Mr. Buchan, one of our usual inmates, returned from Denver with papers, letters for every one but me, and much exciting news. The financial panic has spread out West, gathering strength on its way. The Denver banks have all suspended business. They refuse to cash their own cheques, or to allow their customers to draw a dollar, and would not even give greenbacks for my English gold! Neither Mr. Buchan nor Evans could get a cent. Business is suspended, and everybody, however rich, is for the time being poor.   The Indians have taken to the " war path," and are burning ranches and killing cattle. There is a regular "scare" among the settlers, and waggon loads of fugitives are arriving in Colorado Springs.   The Indians say, "The white man has killed the buffalo and left them to rot on the plains. We will be revenged."   Evans had reached Long-mount, and will be here to-night.

October 10.

"Wait for the waggon" still!   We had a hur-ricane of wind and hail last night; it was eleven before I could go to my cabin, and I only reached it with the help of two men.   The moon was not up, and the sky overhead was black with clouds, when suddenly Long's Peak, which had been invisible, gleamed above the dark mountains, all glistening with new fallen snow, on which the moon, as yet unrisen here, was shining.   The evening before, after sunset, I saw another novel effect.   My lake turned a bril-liant orange in the twilight, and in its still mirror the mountains were reflected a deep rich blue.   It is a world of wonders.   To-day we had a great storm with flurries of fine snow; and when the clouds rolled up at noon, the Snowy Range and all the higher moun-tains were pure white.   I have been hard at work all day to drown my anxieties, which are heightened by a rumour that Evans has gone buffalo-hunting on the Platte!

This evening, quite unexpectedly, Evans arrived with a heavy mail in a box. I sorted it, but there was nothing for me, and Evans said he was afraid that he had left my letters, which were separate from the others, behind at Denver, but he had written from Longmount for them. A few hours later they were found in a box of groceries!

All the hilarity of the house has returned with Evans, and he has brought a kindred spirit with him, a young man who plays and sings splendidly, has an inexhaustible *repertoire*, and produces sonatas, funeral marches, anthems, reels, strathspeys, and all else, out of his wonderful memory. Never, surely, was a chamber organ compelled to such service. A little cask of suspicious appearance was smuggled into the cabin from the waggon, and heightens the hilarity a little, I fear. No churlishness could resist Evans's unutterable jollity or the contagion of his hearty laugh. He claps people on the back, shouts at them, will do anything for them, and makes a perpetual breeze. "My kingdom for a horse!" he has not got one for me, and a shadow crossed his face when I spoke of the subject. Eventually he asked for a private conference, when he told me, with some confusion, that he had found himself "very hard up" in Denver, and had been obliged to appropriate my 100-dollar note. He said he would give me, as interest for it up to November 25th, a good horse, saddle, and bridle for my proposed journey of 600 miles. I was somewhat dismayed, but there was no other course, as the money was gone.[1]   I tried a horse, mended my clothes, reduced my pack to a weight of twelve pounds, and was all ready for an early start, when before daylight I was wakened by Evans's cheery voice at my door. "I say, Miss B., we've got to drive wild cattle to-day; I wish you'd lend a hand, there's not enough of us; I'll give you a good horse; one day won't make much difference." So we've been driving cattle all day, riding about twenty miles, and fording the Big Thompson about as many times. Evans flatters me by saying that I am "as much use as another man;" more than one of our party, I hope, who always avoided the "ugly" cows.

October 12.

I am still here, helping in the kitchen, driving cattle, and riding four or five times a day. Evans detains me each morning by saying, "Here's lots of horses for you to try," and after trying five or six a day, I do not find one to my liking. To-day, as I was cantering a tall well-bred one round the lake, he threw the bridle off by a toss of his head, leaving me with the reins in my hands; one bucked, and two have tender feet, and tumbled down. Such are some of our little varieties. Still I hope to get

[1] In justice to Evans, I must mention here that every cent of the money was ultimately paid, that the horse was perfection, and that the arrangement turned out a most advantageous one for me.

off on my tour in a day or two, so at least as to be able to compare Estes Park with some of the better known parts of Colorado.

You would be amused if you could see our cabin just now. There are nine men in the room and three women. For want of seats most of the men are lying on the floor; all are smoking, and the blithe young French Canadian who plays so beautifully, and catches about fifty speckled trout for each meal, is playing the harmonium with a pipe in his mouth. Three men who have camped in Black Canyon for a week are lying like dogs on the floor. They are all over six feet high, immovably solemn, neither smiling at the general hilarity, nor at the absurd changes which are being rung on the harmonium. They may be described as clothed only in boots, for their clothes are torn to rags. They stare vacantly. They have neither seen a woman nor slept under a roof for six months. Negro songs are being sung, and before that "Yankee Doodle" was played immediately after "Rule Britannia," and it made every one but the strangers laugh, it sounded so foolish and mean. The colder weather is bringing the beasts down from the heights. I heard both wolves and the mountain lion as I crossed to my cabin last night.

                                        I. L. B.

LETTER IX.

" Please Ma'ams"—A Desperado—A Cattle Hunt—The Muster—
A mad Cow—A Snow Storm—Snowed up—Birdie—The Plains
— A Prairie Schooner — Denver — A Find — Plum Creek—
"Being Agreeable"—Snow bound—The Grey Mare.

ESTES PARK, COLORADO.

THIS afternoon, as I was reading in my cabin, little
Sam Edwards ran in, saying, " Mountain Jim wants
to speak to you." This brought to my mind images
of infinite worry, *gauche* servants, " please ma'ams,"
contretemps, and the habit growing out of our elaborate
and uselessly conventional life of magnifying the importance of similar trifles. Then " things " came up,
with the tyranny they exercise. I *really* need nothing
more than this log-cabin offers. But elsewhere one
must have a house and servants, and burdens and
worries—not that one may be hospitable and comfortable, but for the " thick clay " in the shape of
" things " which one has accumulated. My log-house
takes me about five minutes to " do," and you could
eat off the floor, and it needs no lock, as it contains
nothing worth stealing.

But " Mountain Jim " was waiting while I made

these reflections to ask us to take a ride; and he, Mr. and Mrs. Dewy, and I, had a delightful stroll through coloured foliage, and then, when they were fatigued, I changed my horse for his beautiful mare, and we galloped and raced in the beautiful twilight, in the intoxicating, frosty air. Mrs. Dewy wishes you could have seen us as we galloped down the pass, the fearful-looking ruffian on my heavy waggon-horse, and I on his bare wooden saddle, from which beaver, mink, and marten tails, and pieces of skin, were hanging raggedly, with one spur, and feet not in the stirrups, the mare looking so aristocratic and I so beggarly! Mr. Nugent is what is called " splendid company." With a sort of breezy mountain reck-lessness in everything, he passes remarkably acute judgments on men and events; on women also. He has pathos, poetry, and humour, an intense love of nature, strong vanity in certain directions, an obvious desire to act and speak in character, and sustain his reputation as a desperado, a considerable acquaint-ance with literature, a wonderful verbal memory, opinions on every person and subject, a chivalrous respect for women in his manner, which makes it all the more amusing when he suddenly turns round upon one with some graceful raillery, a great power of fascination, and a singular love of children. The children of this house run to him, and when he sits down they climb on his broad shoulders and play with his curls.   They say in the house that "no one who has been here thinks any one worth speaking to after Jim," but I think that this is probably an opinion which time would alter.   Somehow, he is kept always before the public of Colorado, for one can hardly take up a newspaper without finding a paragraph about him, a contribution by him, or a fragment of his biography.   Ruffian as he looks, the first word he speaks—to a lady, at least—places him on a level with educated gentlemen, and his conversation is brilliant, and full of the light and fitfulness of genius.   Yet, on the whole, he is a most painful spectacle.   His magnificent head shows so plainly the better possibilities which might have been his. His life, in spite of a certain dazzle which belongs to it, is a ruined and wasted one, and one asks what of good can the future have in store for one who has for so long chosen evil?[1]

Shall I ever get away?   We were to have had a grand cattle-hunt yesterday, beginning at 6.30, but the horses were all lost.   Often out of fifty horses all that are worth anything are marauding, and a day is lost in hunting for them in the canyons. However, before daylight this morning Evans called through my door, "Miss Bird, I say, we've got to drive cattle fifteen miles, I wish you'd lend a hand;

[1] September of the next year answered the question by laying him down in a dishonoured grave, with a rifle bullet in his brain.

there's not enough of us; I'll give you a good horse."

The scene of the drive is at a height of 7500 feet, watered by two rapid rivers. On all sides mountains rise to an altitude of from 11,000 to 15,000 feet, their skirts shaggy with pitch-pine forests, and scarred by deep canyons, wooded and boulder-strewn, opening upon the mountain pasture previously mentioned. Two thousand head of half-wild Texan cattle are scattered in herds throughout the canyons, living on more or less suspicious terms with grizzly and brown bears, mountain lions, elk, mountain sheep, spotted deer, wolves, lynxes, wild cats, beavers, minks, skunks, chipmonks, eagles, rattlesnakes, and all the other two-legged, four-legged, vertebrate and invertebrate inhabitants of this lonely and romantic region. On the whole, they show a tendency rather to the habits of wild than of domestic cattle. They march to water in Indian file, with the bulls leading, and when threatened, take strategic advantage of ridgy ground, slinking warily along in the hollows, the bulls acting as sentinels, and bringing up the rear in case of an attack from dogs. Cows have to be regularly broken in for milking, being as wild as buffaloes in their unbroken state; but, owing to the comparative dryness of the grasses, and the system of allowing the calf to have the milk during the daytime, a dairy of 200 cows does not produce as much butter as a Devonshire dairy of fifty. Some "necessary" cruelty is involved in the stockman's business, however humane he may be. The system is one of terrorism, and from the time that the calf is bullied into the branding-pen, and the hot iron burns into his shrinking flesh, to the day when the fatted ox is driven down from his boundless pastures to be slaughtered in Chicago, "the fear and dread of man" are upon him.

The herds are apt to penetrate the savage canyons which come down from the Snowy Range, when they incur a risk of being snowed up and starved, and it is necessary now and then to hunt them out and drive them down to the "park." On this occasion, the whole were driven down for a muster, and for the purpose of branding the calves.

After a 6.30 breakfast this morning, we started, the party being composed of my host, a hunter from the Snowy Range, two stockmen from the Plains, one of whom rode a violent buck-jumper, and was said by his comrade to be the "best rider in North Americay," and myself. We were all mounted on Mexican saddles, rode, as the custom is, with light snaffle bridles, leather guards over our feet, and broad wooden stirrups, and each carried his lunch in a pouch slung on the lassoing horn of his saddle. Four big, badly-trained dogs accompanied us. It was a ride of nearly thirty miles, and of many hours, one

of the most splendid I ever took. We never got off
our horses except to tighten the girths, we ate our
lunch with our bridles knotted over our saddle-horns,
started over the level at full gallop, leapt over trunks
of trees, dashed madly down hillsides rugged with
rocks or strewn with great stones, forded deep, rapid
streams, saw lovely lakes and views of surpassing
magnificence, startled a herd of elk with uncouth
heads and monstrous antlers, and in the chase, which
for some time was unsuccessful, rode to the very base
of Long's Peak, over 14,000 feet high, where the
bright waters of one of the affluents of the Platte
burst from the eternal snows through a canyon of
indescribable majesty. The sun was hot, but at a
height of over 8000 feet the air was crisp and frosty,
and the enjoyment of riding a good horse under
such exhilarating circumstances was extreme.   In
one wild part of the ride we had to come down a
steep hill, thickly wooded with pitch-pines, to leap
over the fallen timber, and steer between the dead
and living trees to avoid being " snagged," or bringing down a heavy dead branch by an unwary touch.

Emerging from this, we caught sight of a thousand
Texan cattle feeding in a valley below. The leaders
scented us, and, taking fright, began to move off in
the direction of the open " park," while we were
about a mile from and above them. " Head them
off, boys ! " our leader shouted; " all aboard; hark

away !" and with something of the "High, tally-ho in the morning!" away we all went at a hand-gallop down-hill. I could not hold my excited animal; down-hill, up-hill, leaping over rocks and timber, faster every moment the pace grew, and still the leader shouted, "Go it, boys!" and the horses dashed on at racing speed, passing and repassing each other, till my small but beautiful bay was keeping pace with the immense strides of the great buck-jumper ridden by "the finest rider in North Americay," and I was dizzied and breathless by the pace at which we were going. A shorter time than it takes to tell it brought us close to and abreast of the surge of cattle. The bovine waves were a grand sight : huge bulls, shaped like buffaloes, bellowed and roared, and with great oxen and cows with yearling calves, galloped like racers, and we galloped alongside of them, and shortly headed them, and in no time were placed as sentinels across the mouth of the valley. It seemed like infantry awaiting the shock of cavalry as we stood as still as our excited horses would allow. I almost quailed as the surge came on, but when it got close to us my comrades hooted fearfully, and we dashed forward with the dogs, and, with bellowing, roaring, and thunder of hoofs, the wave receded as it came. I rode up to our leader, who received me with much laughter. He said I was "a good cattle-man," and that he had forgotten that a lady was of

dog as he was swimming, and others, after crossing, headed back in search of some favourite companions which had been left behind, and one specially vicious cow attacked my horse over and over again. It took an hour and a half of time and much patience to gather them all on the other side.

It was getting late in the day, and a snowstorm was impending, before I was joined by the other drivers and herds, and as the former had diminished to three, with only three dogs, it was very difficult to keep the cattle together.   You drive them as gently as possible, so as not to frighten or excite them,[1] riding first on one side, then on the other, to guide them ; and if they deliberately go in a wrong direction, you gallop in front and head them off. The great excitement is when one breaks away from the herd and gallops madly up and down hill, and you

[1] In several visits to America I have observed that the Americans are far in advance of us and our colonial kinsmen in their treatment of horses and other animals. This was very apparent with regard to this Texan herd. There were no stock-whips, no needless worrying of the animals in the excitement of sport. Any dog seizing a bullock by his tail or heels would have been called off and punished, and quietness and gentleness were the rule. The horses were ridden without whips, and with spurs so blunt that they could not hurt even a human skin, and were ruled by the voice and a slight pressure on the light snaffle bridle. This is the usual plan, even where, as in Colorado, the horses are *bronchos*, and inherit ineradicable vice. I never yet saw a horse *bullied* into submission in the United States.

gallop after him anywhere, over and among rocks and trees, doubling when he doubles, and heading him till you get him back again. The bulls were quite easily managed, but the cows with calves, old or young, were most troublesome. By accident I rode between one cow and her calf in a narrow place, and the cow rushed at me and was just getting her big horns under the horse, when he reared, and spun dexterously aside. This kind of thing happened continually. There was one very handsome red cow which became quite mad. She had a calf with her nearly her own size, and thought every one its enemy, and though its horns were well developed, and it was quite able to take care of itself, she insisted on protecting it from all fancied dangers. One of the dogs, a young, foolish thing, seeing that the cow was excited, took a foolish pleasure in barking at her, and she was eventually quite infuriated. She turned to bay forty times at least; tore up the ground with her horns, tossed the great hunting dogs, tossed and killed the calves of two other cows, and finally became so dangerous to the rest of the herd that, just as the drive was ending, Evans drew his revolver and shot her, and the calf for which she had fought so blindly lamented her piteously. She rushed at me several times mad with rage, but these trained cattle-horses keep perfectly cool, and, nearly without will on my part, mine jumped aside at the right moment, and foiled the assailant. Just at dusk we reached the corral—an acre of grass enclosed by stout post-and-rail fences seven feet high, and by much patience and some subtlety lodged the whole herd within its shelter, without a blow, a shout, or even a crack of a whip, wild as the cattle were. It was fearfully cold. We galloped the last mile and a half in four and a half minutes, reached the cabin just as snow began to fall, and found strong, hot tea ready.

October 18.

Snow-bound for three days! I could not write yesterday, it was so awful. People gave up all occupation, and talked of nothing but the storm. The hunters all kept by the great fire in the living-room, only going out to bring in logs and clear the snow from the door and windows. I never spent a more fearful night than two nights ago, alone in my cabin in the storm, with the roof lifting, the mud cracking and coming off, and the fine snow hissing through the chinks between the logs, while splittings and breaking of dead branches, wind-wrung and snow-laden, went on incessantly, with screechings, howlings, thunder and lightning, and many unfamiliar sounds besides. After snowing fiercely all day, another foot of it fell in the early night, and, after drifting against my door, blocked me effectually in. About midnight the mercury fell to zero, and soon after

a gale rose, which lasted for ten hours.   My window
frame is swelled, and shuts, apparently, hermetically;
and my bed is six feet from it.   I had gone to sleep
with six blankets on, and a heavy sheet over my
face.   Between two and three I was awoke by the
cabin being shifted from underneath by the wind,
and the sheet was frozen to my lips.   I put out my
hands, and the bed was thickly covered with fine
snow.   Getting up to investigate matters, I found
the floor some inches deep in parts in fine snow, and
a gust of fine, needle-like snow stung my face.   The
bucket of water was solid ice.   I lay in bed freezing
till sunrise, when some of the men came to see if I
"was alive," and to dig me out.   They brought a
can of hot water, which turned to ice before I could
use it.   I dressed standing in snow, and my brushes,
boots, and etceteras were covered with snow.   When
I ran to the house, not a mountain or anything else
could be seen, and the snow on one side was drifted
higher than the roof.   The air, as high as one could
see, was one white, stinging smoke of snow-drift—a
terrific sight.   In the living-room, the snow was
driving through the chinks, and Mrs. Dewy was
shovelling it from the floor.   Mr. D.'s beard was
hoary with frost in a room with a fire all night.
Evans was lying ill, with his bed covered with snow.
Returning from my cabin after breakfast, loaded
with occupations for the day, I was lifted off my

feet, and deposited in a drift, and all my things, writing-book and letter included, were carried in different directions. Some, including a valuable photograph, are irrecoverable. The writing-book was found, some hours afterwards, under three feet of snow.

There are tracks of bears and deer close to the house, but no one can hunt in this gale, and the drift is blinding. We have been slightly overcrowded in our one room. Chess, music, and whist have been resorted to. One hunter, for very *ennui*, has devoted himself to keeping my ink from freezing. We all sat in great cloaks and coats, and kept up an enormous fire, with the pitch running out of the logs. The isolation is extreme, for we are literally snowed-up, and the other settler in the Park and "Mountain Jim" are both at Denver. Late in the evening the storm ceased. In some places the ground is bare of snow, while in others all irregularities are levelled, and the drifts are forty feet deep. Nature is grand under this new aspect. The cold is awful; the high wind with the mercury at zero would skin any part exposed to it.

October 19.

Evans offers me six dollars a week if I will stay into the winter and do the cooking after Mrs. Edwards leaves! I think I should like playing at being a "hired girl" if it were not for the bread-making! But it would suit me better to ride

after cattle. The men don't like "baching," as it is
called in the wilds—*i.e.* "doing for themselves."
They washed and ironed their clothes yesterday, and
there was an incongruity about the last performance.
I really think (though for the fifteenth time) that I
shall leave to-morrow. The cold has moderated, the
sky is bluer than ever, the snow is evaporating, and
a hunter who has joined us to-day says that there are
no drifts on the trail which one cannot get through.

LONGMOUNT, COLORADO, *October 20.*

"The Island Valley of Avillon" is left, but how
shall I finally tear myself from its freedom and en-
chantments? I see Long's snowy peak rising into the
night sky, and know and long after the magnificence
of the blue hollow at its base. We were to have left
at 8, but the horses were lost, so it was 9.30 before
we started, the *we* being the musical young French
Canadian and myself. I have a bay Indian pony,
"Birdie," a little beauty, with legs of iron, fast,
enduring, gentle, and wise; and with luggage for
some weeks, including a black silk dress, behind my
saddle, I am tolerably independent. It was a most
glorious ride. We passed through the gates of rock,
through gorges where the unsunned snow lay deep
under the lemon-coloured aspens; caught glimpses of
far-off, snow-clad giants rising into a sky of deep sad
blue; lunched above the Foot Hills at a cabin where

two brothers and a "hired man" were "keeping bach," where everything was so trim, clean, and ornamental that one did not miss a woman; crossed a deep backwater on a narrow beaver-dam, because the log bridge was broken down, and emerged from the brilliantly-coloured canyon of the St. Vrain just at dusk upon the featureless prairies, when we had some trouble in finding Longmount in the dark. A hospitable welcome awaited me at this inn, and an English friend came in and spent the evening with me.

GREAT PLATTE CANYON, *October 23.*

My letters on this tour will, I fear, be very dull, for after riding all day, looking after my pony, getting supper, hearing about various routes, and the pastoral, agricultural, mining, and hunting gossip of the neighbourhood, I am so sleepy and wholesomely tired that I can hardly write. I left Longmount pretty early on Tuesday morning, the day being sad, with the blink of an impending snowstorm in the air. The evening before I was introduced to a man who had been a colonel in the rebel army, who made a most unfavourable impression upon me, and it was a great annoyance to me when he presented himself on horseback to guide me "over the most intricate part of the journey." Solitude is infinitely preferable to uncongeniality, and is bliss when compared with repulsiveness, so I was thoroughly glad when I got rid of my

escort and set out upon the prairie alone. It is a
dreary ride of thirty miles over the low brown plains
to Denver, very little settled, and with trails going
in all directions. My sailing orders were "steer
south, and keep to the best-beaten track," and it
seemed like embarking on the ocean without a compass. The rolling brown waves on which you see a
horse a mile and a half off impress one strangely, and
at noon the sky darkened up for another storm, the
mountains swept down in blackness to the Plains,
and the higher peaks took on a ghastly grimness
horrid to behold. It was first very cold, then very
hot, and finally settled down to a fierce east-windy
cold, difficult to endure. It was free and breezy,
however, and my horse was companionable. Sometimes herds of cattle were browsing on the sun-cured
grass, then herds of horses. Occasionally I met a
horseman with a rifle lying across his saddle, or a
waggon of the ordinary sort, but oftener I saw a
waggon with a white tilt, of the kind known as a
"Prairie Schooner," labouring across the grass, or a
train of them, accompanied by herds, mules, and
horsemen, bearing emigrants and their household
goods in dreary exodus from the Western States to
the much-vaunted prairies of Colorado. The host
and hostess of one of these waggons invited me to
join their mid-day meal, I providing tea (which they
had not tasted for four weeks) and they hominy.

They had been three months on the journey from Illinois, and their oxen were so lean and weak that they expected to be another month in reaching Wet Mountain Valley. They had buried a child *en route*, had lost several oxen, and were rather out of heart. Owing to their long isolation and the monotony of the march they had lost count of events, and seemed like people of another planet. They wanted me to join them, but their rate of travel was too slow, so we parted with mutual expressions of goodwill, and as their white tilt went " hull down " in the distance on the lonely prairie sea, I felt sadder than I often feel on taking leave of old acquaintances. That night they must have been nearly frozen, camping out in the deep snow in the fierce wind. I met afterwards 2000 lean Texan cattle, herded by three wild-looking men on horseback, followed by two waggons containing women, children, and rifles. They had travelled 1000 miles. Then I saw two prairie wolves, like jackals, with gray fur, cowardly creatures, which fled from me with long leaps.

The windy cold became intense, and for the next eleven miles I rode a race with the coming storm. At the top of every prairie roll I expected to see Denver, but it was not till nearly five that from a considerable height I looked down upon the great " City of the Plains," the " Metropolis of the Territories." There the great braggart city lay spread out, brown and treeless, upon the brown and treeless plain, which seemed to nourish nothing but wormwood and the Spanish bayonet. The shallow Platte, shrivelled into a narrow stream with a shingly bed six times too large for it, and fringed by shrivelled cotton-wood, wound along by Denver, and two miles up its course I saw a great sand-storm, which in a few minutes covered the city, blotting it out with a dense brown cloud. Then with gusts of wind the snow-storm began, and I had to trust entirely to Birdie's sagacity for finding Evans's shantie. She had been there once before only, but carried me direct to it over rough ground and trenches. Gleefully Mrs. Evans and the children ran out to welcome the pet pony, and I was received most hospitably, and made warm and comfortable, though the house consists only of a kitchen and two bed-closets. My budget of news from "the Park" had to be brought out constantly, and I wondered how much I had to tell. It was past eleven when we breakfasted the next morning. It was cloudless and an intense frost, with six inches of snow on the ground, and everybody thought it too cold to get up and light the fire. I had intended to leave Birdie at Denver, but ex-Governor Hunt and Mr. Byers of the *Rocky Mountain News* both advised me to travel on horseback rather than by train and stage, telling me that I should be quite safe, and ex-Governor Hunt drew out a route for me and gave me a circular letter to the settlers along it.

Denver is no longer the Denver of Hepworth Dixon. A shooting affray in the street is as rare as in Liverpool, and one no longer sees men dangling to the lamp-posts when one looks out in the morning! It is a busy place, the *entrepôt* and distributing-point for an immense district, with good shops, some factories, fair hotels, and the usual deformities and refinements of civilisation. Peltry shops abound, and sportsman, hunter, miner, teamster, emigrant, can be completely rigged out at fifty different stores. At Denver, people who come from the east to try the "camp cure," now so fashionable, get their outfit of waggon, driver, horses, tent, bedding, and stove, and start for the mountains. Asthmatic people are there in such numbers as to warrant the holding of an "asthmatic convention" of patients cured and benefited. Numbers of invalids who cannot bear the rough life of the mountains fill its hotels and boarding-houses, and others who have been partially restored by a summer of camping out, go into the city in the winter to complete the cure. It stands at a height of 5000 feet, on an enormous plain, and has a most glorious view of the Rocky Range. I should hate even to spend a week there. The sight of those glories so near and yet out of reach would make me nearly crazy. Denver is at present the terminus of the Kansas Pacific Railroad. It has a line connecting it with the Union Pacific Railroad at Cheyenne, and by means of the Denver and Rio Grande Railroad, open for about 200 miles, it is expecting to reach into Mexico. It has also had the enterprise, by means of another narrow-gauge railroad, to push its way right up into the mining districts near Gray's Peak. The number of "saloons" in the streets impresses one, and everywhere one meets the characteristic loafers of a frontier town, who find it hard even for a few days or hours to submit to the restraints of civilisation, as hard as I did to ride sidewise to ex-Governor Hunt's office. To Denver men go to spend the savings of months of hard work in the maddest dissipation, and there such characters as "Comanche Bill," "Buffalo Bill," "Wild Bill," and "Mountain Jim," go on the spree, and find the kind of notoriety they seek. A large number of Indians added to the harlequin appearance of the Denver streets the day I was there. They belonged to the Ute tribe, through which I had to pass, and ex-Governor Hunt introduced me to a fine-looking young chief, very well dressed in beaded hide, and bespoke his courtesy for me if I needed it. The Indian stores and fur stores and fur depôts interested me most. The crowds in the streets, perhaps owing to the snow on the ground, were almost solely masculine. I only saw five women the whole day. There were men in every rig : hunters and trappers in buckskin clothing ; men of the Plains with belts and revolvers, in great blue cloaks, relics of the war ; teamsters in leathern suits ; horsemen in fur

coats and caps and buffalo-hide boots with the hair
outside, and camping blankets behind their huge
Mexican saddles; Broadway dandies in light kid
gloves; rich English sporting tourists, clean, comely,
and supercilious-looking; and hundreds of Indians on
their small ponies, the men wearing buckskin suits
sewn with beads, and red blankets, with faces painted
vermilion, and hair hanging lank and straight, and
squaws much bundled up, riding astride with furs
over their saddles.

Town tired and confused me, and in spite of Mrs.
Evans's kind hospitality, I was glad when a man
brought Birdie at nine yesterday morning.   He said
she was a little demon, she had done nothing but
buck, and had bucked him off on the bridge!   I found
that he had put a curb on her, and whenever she dis-
likes anything she resents it by bucking.   I rode sidewise till I was well through the town, long enough to
produce a severe pain in my spine, which was not
relieved for some time even after I had changed my
position.   It was a lovely Indian summer day, so
warm that the snow on the ground looked an incongruity.   I rode over the Plains for some time, then
gradually reached the rolling country along the base
of the mountains, and a stream with cotton-woods
along it, and settlers' houses about every half-mile.
I passed and met waggons frequently, and picked up
a muff containing a purse with five hundred dollars
in it, which I afterwards had the great pleasure of

restoring to the owner.   Several times I crossed the narrow track of the quaint little Rio Grande Railroad, so that it was a very cheerful ride.

RANCH, PLUM CREEK, *October 24.*

You must understand that in Colorado travel, unless on the main road and in the larger settlements, there are neither hotels nor taverns, and that it is the custom for the settlers to receive travellers, charging them at the usual hotel rate for accommodation.   It is a very satisfactory arrangement.   However, at Ranch, my first halting-place, the host was unwilling to receive people in this way, I afterwards found, or I certainly should not have presented my credentials at the door of a large frame house, with large barns and a generally prosperous look.   The host, who opened the door, looked repellant, but his wife, a very agreeable, lady-like-looking woman, said they could give me a bed on a sofa.   The house was the most pretentious I have yet seen, being papered and carpeted, and there were two "hired girls."   There was a lady there from Laramie, who kindly offered to receive me into her room, a very tall, elegant person, remarkable as being the first woman who had settled in the Rocky Mountains.   She had been trying the "camp cure" for three months, and was then on her way home.   She had a waggon with beds, tent, tent-floor, cooking-stove, and every camp luxury, a light buggy, a man to manage everything, and a most superior "hired girl." She was consumptive and frail in strength, but a very attractive person, and her stories of the perils and limitations of her early life at Fort Laramie were very interesting. Still I "wearied," as I had arrived early in the afternoon, and could not out of politeness retire and write to you. At meals the three "hired men" and two "hired girls" eat with the family. I soon found that there was a screw loose in the house, and was glad to leave early the next morning, although it was obvious that a storm was coming on. I saw the toy car of the Rio Grande Railroad whirl past, all cushioned and warmed, and rather wished I were in it, and not out among the snow on the bleak hill-side. I only got on four miles when the storm came on so badly that I got into a kitchen where eleven wretched travellers were taking shelter, with the snow melting on them and dripping on the floor. I had learned the art of "being agreeable" so well at the Chalmers's, and practised it so successfully during the two hours I was there, by paring potatoes and making scones, that when I left, though the hosts kept "an accommodation house for travellers," they would take nothing for my entertainment, because they said I was such "good company"! The storm moderated a little, and at one I saddled Birdie, and rode four more miles, crossing a frozen creek, the ice of which broke and let the pony through, to her great alarm. I cannot describe my feelings on this ride, produced by the utter loneliness, the silence and dumbness of all

LETTER X.

A White World—Bad Travelling—A Millionaire's Home—Pleasant
Park—Perry's Park—Stock-raising—A Cattle King—The
Arkansas Divide—Birdie's Sagacity—Luxury—Monument
Park—Deference to Prejudice—A Death Scene—The Manitou—
A loose Shoe—The Ute Pass—Bergens Park—A Settler's Home
—Hayden's Divide—Sharp Criticism—Speaking the truth.

COLORADO SPRINGS, *October 28.*

IT is difficult to make this anything of a letter. I
have been riding for a whole week, seeing wonders
and greatly enjoying the singular adventurousness
and novelty of my tour, but ten hours or more daily
spent in the saddle in this rarefied, intoxicating air,
disposes one to sleep rather than to write in the evening, and is far from conducive to mental brilliancy.
The observing faculties are developed, and the reflec-
tive lie dormant.

That night on which I last wrote was the coldest
I have yet felt. I pulled the rag carpet from the
floor and covered myself with it, but could not get
warm. The sun rose gloriously on a shrouded earth.
Barns, road, shrubs, fences, river, lake, all lay under
the glittering snow. It was light and powdery, and

sparkled like diamonds. Not a breath of wind stirred, there was not a sound. I had to wait till a passing horseman had broken the track, but soon after I set off into the new, shining world. I soon lost the horseman's footmarks, but kept on near the road by means of the innumerable footprints of birds and ground squirrels, which all went in one direction. After riding for an hour I was obliged to get off and walk for another, for the snow balled in Birdie's feet to such an extent that she could hardly keep up even without my weight on her, and my pick was not strong enough to remove it. Turning off the road to ask for a chisel, I came upon the cabin of the people whose muff I had picked up a few days before, and they received me very warmly, gave me a tumbler of cream, and made some strong coffee. They were " old country folk," and I stayed too long with them. After leaving them I rode twelve miles, but it was " bad travelling," from the balling of the snow and the difficulty of finding the track. There was a fearful loneliness about it. The track was untrodden, and I saw neither man nor beast. The sky became densely clouded, and the outlook was awful. The great Divide of the Arkansas was in front, looming vaguely through a heavy snow-cloud, and snow began to fall, not in powder, but in heavy flakes. Finding that there would be risk in trying to ride till nightfall, in the early afternoon I left the road and went two miles into the hills by an untrodden path, where there were gates to open and a rapid steep-sided creek to cross; and at the entrance to a most fantastic gorge I came upon an elegant frame house belonging to Mr. Perry, a millionaire, to whom I had an introduction, which I did not hesitate to present, as it was weather in which a traveller might almost ask for shelter without one.

Mr. Perry was away, but his daughter, a very bright-looking, elegantly-dressed girl, invited me to dine and remain. They had stewed venison and various luxuries on the table, which was tasteful and refined, and an adroit, coloured table-maid waited, one of five attached negro servants who had been their slaves before the war. After dinner, though snow was slowly falling, a gentleman cousin took me a ride to show me the beauties of Pleasant Park, which takes rank among the finest scenery of Colorado, and in good weather is very easy of access. It did look very grand as we entered it by a narrow pass guarded by two buttes, or isolated upright masses of rock, bright red, and about 300 feet in height. The pines were very large, and the narrow canyons which came down on the Park gloomily magnificent. It is remarkable also from a quantity of "monumental" rocks, from 50 to 300 feet in height, bright vermilion, green, buff, orange, and sometimes all combined, their gay tinting a contrast to the disastrous-looking snow and the sombre pines. Bear Canyon, a gorge of singular majesty, comes down on the Park, and we crossed the Bear Creek at the foot of this on the ice, which gave way, and both our horses broke through into pretty deep and very cold water, and shortly afterwards Birdie put her foot into a prairie dog's hole which was concealed by the snow, and on recovering herself fell three times on her nose. I thought of Bishop Wilberforce's fatal accident from a smaller stumble, and felt sure that he would have kept his seat had he been mounted, as I was, on a Mexican saddle. It was too threatening for a long ride, and on returning I passed into a region of vivacious descriptions of Egypt, Palestine, Asia Minor, Turkey, Russia, and other countries, in which Miss Perry had travelled with her family for three years.

[Perry's Park is one of the great cattle-raising ranches in Colorado. This, the youngest State in the Union, a Territory until quite recently, has an area of about 68,000,000 acres, a great portion of which, though rich in mineral wealth, is worthless either for stock or arable farming, and the other or eastern part is so dry that crops can only be grown profitably where irrigation is possible. This region is watered by the south fork of the Platte and its affluents, and, though subject to the grasshopper pest, it produces wheat of the finest quality, the yield varying according to the mode of cultivation from 18 to 30 bushels per acre. The necessity for irrigation, however, will always bar the way to an indefinite extension of the area of arable farms. The prospects of cattle-raising seem at present practically unlimited. In 1876 Colorado had 390,728, valued at £2 : 13s. per head, about half of which were imported as young beasts from Texas. The climate is so fine and the pasturage so ample that shelter and hand-feeding are never resorted to except in the case of imported breeding stock from the Eastern States, which sometimes in severe winters need to be fed in sheds for a short time. Mr. Perry devotes himself mainly to the breeding of graded shorthorn bulls, which he sells when young for £6 per head.

The cattle run at large upon the prairies; each animal being branded, they need no herding, and are usually only mustered, counted, and the increase branded in the summer. In the fall, when three or four years old, they are sold lean or in tolerable condition to dealers who take them by rail to Chicago, or elsewhere, where the fattest lots are slaughtered for tinning or for consumption in the Eastern cities, while the leaner are sold to farmers for feeding up during the winter. Some of the wealthier stockmen take their best lots to Chicago themselves. The Colorado cattle are either pure Texan or Spanish, or crosses between the Texan and graded shorthorns. They are nearly all very inferior animals, being bony and ragged. The herds mix on the vast plains at will; along the Arkansas valley 80,000 roam about with the freedom of buffaloes, and of this number about 16,000 are exported every fall. Where cattle are killed for use in the mining districts their average price is 3 cents per lb. In the summer thousands of yearlings are driven up from Texas, branded, and turned loose on the prairies, and are not molested again till they are sent east at three or four years old. These pure Texans, the old Spanish breed, weigh from 900 to 1000 pounds, and the crossed Colorado cattle from 1000 to 1200 pounds.

The "Cattle King" of the State is Mr. Iliff, of South Platte, who owns nine ranches, with runs of 15,000 acres, and 35,000 cattle. He is improving his herd rapidly by means of imported shorthorn stock; and, indeed, the opening of the dead-meat trade with this country is giving a great impetus to the improvement of the breed of cattle among all the larger and richer stock-owners. For this enormous herd 40 men are employed in summer, about 12 in winter, and 200 horses. In the rare case of a severe and protracted snow-storm the cattle get a little hay. Owners of 6000, 8000, and 10,000 head of cattle are quite common in Colorado. Sheep are now raised in the State to the extent of half a million, and a chronic feud prevails between the "sheep men" and the "cattle men." Sheep-raising is said to be a very profitable

business, but its risks and losses are greater, owing
to storms, while the outlay for labour, dipping
materials, etc., is considerably larger, and owing to
the comparative inability of sheep to scratch away
the snow from the grass, hay has to be provided to
meet the emergency of very severe snow-storms.
The flocks are made up mostly of pure and graded
Mexicans; but though some flocks which have been
graded carefully for some years show considerable
merit, the average sheep is a leggy, ragged beast.
Wether mutton, four and five years old, is sold when
there is any demand for it; but except at Charpiot's,
in Denver, I never saw mutton on any table, public
or private, and wool is the great source of profit, the
old ewes being allowed to die off. The best flocks
yield an average of seven pounds of wool, and the
worst two and a half pounds. The shearing season,
which begins in early June, lasts about six weeks.
Shearers get six and a half cents a head for inferior
sheep, and seven and a half for the better quality,
and a good hand shears from sixty to eighty in a day.
It is not likely that sheep-raising will attain anything
of the prominence which cattle-raising is likely to
assume. The potato-beetle "scare" is not of much
account in the country of the potato-beetle. The
farmers seem much more depressed by the magni-
tude and persistency of the grasshopper pest, which
finds their fields in the morning "as the garden of

cunning head and looked at me. It was useless to argue the point with so sagacious a beast. To the right of the bridge the ice was much broken, and we forded the river there; but as it was deep enough to come up to her body, and was icy cold to my feet, I wondered at her preference. Afterwards I heard that the bridge was dangerous. She is the queen of ponies, and is very gentle, though she has not only wild horse blood, but is herself the wild horse. She is always cheerful and hungry, never tired, looks intelligently at everything, and her legs are like rocks. Her one trick is that when the saddle is put on she swells herself to a very large size, so that if any one not accustomed to her saddles her I soon find the girth three or four inches too large. When I saddle her, a gentle slap on her side, or any slight start which makes her cease to hold her breath, puts it all right. She is quite a companion, and bathing her back, sponging her nostrils, and seeing her fed after my day's ride, is always my first care.

At last I reached a log cabin where I got a feed for us both and further directions. The rest of the day's ride was awful enough. The snow was thirteen inches deep, and grew deeper as I ascended in silence and loneliness, but just as the sun sank behind a snowy peak I reached the top of the Divide, 7975 feet above the sea-level. There, in unspeakable solitude, lay a frozen lake. Owls hooted among the pines, the trail was obscure, the country was not settled, the mercury was 9° below zero, my feet had lost all sensation, and one of them was frozen to the wooden stirrup. I found that owing to the depth of the snow I had only ridden fifteen miles in eight and a half hours, and must look about for a place to sleep in. The eastern sky was unlike anything I ever saw before. It had been chrysoprase, then it turned to aquamarine, and that to the bright full green of an emerald. Unless I am colour-blind, this is true. Then suddenly the whole changed, and flushed with the pure, bright, rose-colour of the afterglow. Birdie was sliding at every step, and I was nearly paralysed with the cold when I reached a cabin which had been mentioned to me, but they said that seventeen snow-bound men were lying on the floor, and they advised me to ride half a mile farther, which I did, and reached the house of a German from Eisenau, with a sweet young wife and a venerable mother-in-law. Though the house was very poor, it was made attractive by ornaments, and the simple, loving, German ways gave it a sweet home atmosphere. My room was reached by a ladder, but I had it to myself and had the luxury of a basin to wash in. Under the kindly treatment of the two women my feet came to themselves, but with an amount of pain that almost deserved the name of torture.

The next morning was gray and sour, but bright-

ened and warmed as the day went on.   After riding
twelve miles I got bread and milk for myself and a
feed for Birdie at a large house where there were eight
boarders, each one looking nearer the grave than the
other, and on remounting was directed to leave the
main road and diverge through Monument Park, a
ride of twelve miles among fantastic rocks, but I lost
my way, and came to an end of all tracks in a wild
canyon.   Returning about six miles, I took another
track, and rode about eight miles without seeing a
creature.   I then came to strange gorges with wonderful upright rocks of all shapes and colours, and turning through a gate of rock, came upon what I knew
must be Glen Eyrie, as wild and romantic a glen as
imagination ever pictured.   The track then passed
down a valley close under some ghastly peaks, wild,
cold, awe-inspiring scenery.   After fording a creek
several times, I came upon a decayed-looking cluster
of houses bearing the arrogant name of Colorado City,
and two miles farther on, from the top of one of the
Foot Hill ridges, I saw the bleak-looking scattered
houses of the ambitious watering-place of Colorado
Springs, the goal of my journey of 150 miles.   I got
off, put on a long skirt, and rode sidewise, though the
settlement scarcely looked like a place where any
deference to prejudices was necessary.   A queer
embryo-looking place it is, out on the bare Plains,
yet it is rising and likely to rise, and has some big

mysterious door as plainly as I did. All this time, and during the movings in the room, I saw two large white feet sticking up at the end of the bed. I watched and watched, hoping those feet would move, but they did not; and somehow, to my thinking, they grew stiffer and whiter, and then my horrible suspicion deepened, that while we were sitting there a human spirit untended and desolate had passed forth into the night. Then a man came out with a bundle of clothes, and then the sick young man, groaning and sobbing, and then a third, who said to me, with some feeling, that the man who had just died was the sick young man's only brother. And still the landlady laughed and talked, and afterwards said to me, " It turns the house upside down when they just come here and die; we shall be half the night laying him out." I could not sleep for the bitter cold and the sound of the sobs and groans of the bereaved brother. The next day the landlady, in a fashionably-made black dress, was bustling about, proud of the prospective arrival of a handsome coffin. I went into the parlour to get a needle, and the door of *that* room was open, and children were running in and out, and the landlady, who was sweeping there, called cheerily to me to come in for the needle, and there, to my horror, not even covered with a face-cloth, and with the sun blazing in through the unblinded window, lay that thing of terror, a corpse, on some chairs which were

the names of which are familiar to every one—the
Garden of the Gods, Glen Eyrie, Pike's Peak, Monument Park, and the Ute Pass.   It has two or three
immense hotels, and a few houses picturesquely situated.   It is thronged by thousands of people in the
summer who come to drink the waters, try the camp
cure, and make mountain excursions; but it is all
quiet now, and there are only a few lingerers in this
immense hotel.   There is a rushing torrent in a
valley, with mountains, covered with snow and rising
to a height of nearly 15,000 feet, overhanging it.   It
is grand and awful, and has a strange, solemn beauty
like death.   And the Snowy Mountains are pierced
by the torrent which has excavated the Ute Pass, by
which, to-morrow, I hope to go into the higher regions.
But all may be "lost for want of a horseshoe-nail."
One of Birdie's shoes is loose, and not a nail is to be
got here, or can be got till I have ridden for ten miles
up the Pass.   Birdie amuses every one with her
funny ways.   She always follows me closely, and
to-day got quite into a house and pushed the parlour-
door open.   She walks after me with her head laid
on my shoulder, licking my face and teasing me for
sugar; and sometimes, when any one else takes hold
of her, she rears and kicks, and the vicious *broncho*
soul comes into her eyes.   Her face is cunning and
pretty, and she makes a funny, blarneying noise when
I go up to her.   The men at all the stables make a

hotel, I came here to have a last taste of luxury. They charge six dollars a day in the season, but it is now half-price; and instead of four hundred fashionable guests there are only fifteen, most of whom are speaking in the weak, rapid accents of consumption, and are coughing their hearts out.   There are seven medicinal springs.   It is strange to have the luxuries of life in my room.   It will be only the fourth night in Colorado that I have slept on anything better than hay or straw.   I am glad that there are so few inns.   As it is, I get a good deal of insight into the homes and modes of living of the settlers.

BERGENS PARK, *October 31.*

This cabin was so dark, and I so sleepy last night, that I could not write; but the frost during the night has been very severe, and I am detained until the bright, hot sun melts the ice and renders travelling safe. I left the great Manitou at ten yesterday. Birdie, who was loose in the stable, came trotting down the middle of it when she saw me for her sugar and biscuits. No nails could be got, and her shoe was hanging by two, which doomed me to a foot's-pace and the dismal clink of a loose shoe for three hours.   There was not a cloud on the bright blue sky the whole day, and though it froze hard in the shade, it was summer-heat in the sun.   The mineral fountains were sparkling in their basins and sending up their full perennial jets;

but the snow-clad, pine-skirted mountains frowned and darkened over the Ute Pass as I entered it to ascend it for twenty miles. A narrow pass it is, with barely room for the torrent and the waggon road which has been blasted out of its steep sides. All the time I was in sight of the Fountain river, brighter than any stream, because it tumbles over rose-red granite, rocky or disintegrated, a truly fair stream, cutting and forcing its way through hard rocks, under arches of alabaster ice, through fringes of crystalline ice, thumping with a hollow sound in cavernous recesses cold and dark, or leaping in foam from heights with rush and swish; always bright and riotous, never pausing in still pools to rest, dashing through gates of rock, pine-hung, pine-bridged, pine-buried; twinkling and laughing in the sunshine, or frowning in "dowie dens" in the blue pine gloom. And there, for a mile or two in a sheltered spot, owing to the more southern latitude, the everlasting northern pine met the trees of other climates. There were dwarf oaks, willows, hazel, and spruce; the white cedar and the trailing juniper jostled each other for a precarious foothold; the majestic redwood-tree of the Pacific met the exquisite balsam-pine of the Atlantic slopes, and among them all the pale gold foliage of the large aspen trembled (as the legend goes) in endless remorse. And above them towered the toothy peaks of the glittering mountains, rising in pure white against the

sunny blue.   Grand! glorious! sublime! but not
lovable.   I would give all for the luxurious redun-
dance of one Hilo gulch, or for one day of those soft
dreamy " skies whose very tears are balm."

Up ever! the road being blasted out of the red
rock which often overhung it, the canyon only from
fifteen to twenty feet wide, the thunder of the Fountain, which is crossed eight times, nearly deafening.
Sometimes the sun struck the road, and then it was
absolutely hot; then one entered unsunned gorges
where the snow lay deep, and the crowded pines made
dark twilight, and the river roared under ice bridges
fringed by icicles.   At last the Pass opened out upon
a sunlit upland Park, where there was a forge, and
with Birdie's shoe put on, and some shoenails in my
purse, I rode on cheerfully, getting food for us both at
a ranch belonging to some very pleasant people, who,
like all Western folk, when they are not taciturn,
asked a legion of questions.   There I met a Colonel
Kittridge, who said that he believed his valley, twelve
miles off the track, to be the loveliest valley in Colorado, and invited me to his house.   Leaving the road,
I went up a long ascent deep in snow, but as it did
not seem to be the way, I tied up the pony, and walked
on to a cabin at some distance, which I had hardly
reached when I found her trotting like a dog by my
side, pulling my sleeve and laying her soft gray nose
on my shoulder.   Does it all mean sugar ?   We had

eight miles farther to go—most of the way through a
forest, which I always dislike when alone, from the
fear of being frightened by something which may
appear from behind a tree. I saw a beautiful white
fox, several skunks, some chipmonks and gray squirrels, owls, crows, and crested blue-jays. As the sun
was getting low I reached Bergens Park, which was
to put me out of conceit with Estes Park. Never!
It is long and featureless, and its immediate surroundings are mean. It reminded me in itself of some dismal Highland strath—Glenshee, possibly. I looked
at it with special interest, as it was the place at which
Miss Kingsley had suggested that I might remain.
The evening was glorious, and the distant views were
very fine. A stream fringed with cotton-wood runs
through the Park; low ranges come down upon it.
The south end is completely closed up, but at a considerable distance, by the great mass of Pike's Peak,
while far beyond the other end are peaks and towers,
wonderful in blue and violet in the lovely evening,
and beyond these, sharply defined against the clear
green sky, was the serrated ridge of the Snowy Range,
said to be 200 miles away. Bergens Park has been
bought by Dr. Bell, of London, but its present occu-
pant is Mr. Thornton, an English gentleman, who has
a worthy married Englishman as his manager. Mr.
Thornton is building a good house, and purposes to
build other cabins, with the intention of making the

Park a resort for strangers. I thought of the blue hollow lying solitary at the foot of Long's Peak, and rejoiced that I had "happened into it."

The cabin is long, low, mud-roofed, and very dark. The middle place is full of raw meat, fowls, and gear. One end, almost dark, contains the cooking-stove, milk, crockery, a long deal table, two benches, and some wooden stools; the other end houses the English manager or partner, his wife, and three children, another cooking-stove, gear of all kinds, and sacks of beans and flour. They put up a sheet for a partition, and made me a shake-down on the gravel floor of this room. Ten hired men sat down to meals with us. It was all very rough, dark, and comfortless, but Mr. T., who is not only a gentleman by birth, but an M.A. of Cambridge, seems to like it. Much in this way (a little smoother if a lady is in the case) every man must begin life here. Seven large dogs—three of them with cats upon their backs — are usually warming themselves at the fire.

TWIN ROCK, SOUTH FORK OF THE PLATTE, *November 1.*

I did not leave Mr. Thornton's till ten, because of the slipperiness. I rode four miles along a back trail, and then was so tired that I stayed for two hours at a ranch, where I heard, to my dismay, that I must ride twenty-four miles farther before I could find any place to sleep at. I did not enjoy yester-

day's ride. I was both tired and rheumatic, and
Birdie was not so sprightly as usual. After starting
again I came on a hideous place, of which I had not
heard before, Hayden's Divide, one of the great back-
bones of the region, a weary expanse of deep snow
eleven miles across, and fearfully lonely. I saw
nothing the whole way but a mule lately dead lying
by the road. I was very nervous somehow, and
towards evening believed that I had lost the road,
for I came upon wild pine forests, with huge masses
of rock from 100 to 700 feet high, cast here and
there among them; beyond these pine-sprinkled
grass hills; these, in their turn, were bounded by
interminable ranges, ghastly in the lurid evening,
with the Spanish Peaks quite clear, and the colossal
summit of Mount Lincoln, the King of the Rocky
Mountains, distinctly visible, though seventy miles
away. It seemed awful to be alone on that ghastly
ridge, surrounded by interminable mountains, in the
deep snow, knowing that a party of thirty had been
lost here a month ago. Just at nightfall the descent
of a steep hill took me out of the forest and upon a
clean log cabin, where, finding that the proper halting-
place was two miles farther on, I remained. A truly
pleasing, superior-looking woman placed me in a
rocking-chair; would not let me help her otherwise
than by rocking the cradle, and made me "feel at
home." The room, though it serves them and their

two children for kitchen, parlour, and bedroom, is the pattern of brightness, cleanliness, and comfort. At supper there were canned raspberries, rolls, butter, tea, venison, and fried rabbit, and at seven I went to bed in a carpeted log room, with a thick feather-bed on a mattress, sheets, ruffled pillow slips, and a pile of warm white blankets! I slept for eleven hours. They discourage me much about the route which ex-Governor Hunt has projected for me. They think that it is impassable, owing to snow, and that another storm is brewing.

HALLS GULCH, *November 6.*

I have ridden 150 miles since I wrote last. On leaving Twin Rock on Saturday I had a short day's ride to Colonel Kittridge's cabin at Oil Creek, where I spent a quiet Sunday with agreeable people. The ride was all through parks and gorges, and among pine-clothed hills, about 9000 feet high, with Pike's Peak always in sight. I have developed much sagacity in finding a trail, or I should not be able to make use of such directions as these: "Keep along a gulch four or five miles till you get Pike's Peak on your left, then follow some wheel-marks till you get to some timber, and keep to the north till you come to a creek, where you'll find a great many elk tracks; then go to your right and cross the creek three times, then you'll see a red rock to your left," etc. etc. The K.'s cabin was very small and lonely, and the life seemed a hard grind for an educated and refined woman. There were snow flurries after I arrived, but the first Sunday of November was as bright and warm as June, and the atmosphere had resumed its exquisite purity. Three peaks of Pike's Peak are seen from Oil Creek, above the nearer hills, and by them they tell the time. We had been in the evening shadows for half an hour before those peaks ceased to be transparent gold. On leaving Colonel Kittridge's hospitable cabin I dismounted, as I had often done before, to lower a bar, and, on looking round, Birdie was gone! I spent an hour in trying to catch her, but she had taken an "ugly fit," and would not let me go near her; and I was getting tired and vexed, when two passing trappers, on mules, circumvented and caught her. I rode the twelve miles back to Twin Rock, and then went on, a kindly teamster, who was going in the same direction, taking my pack. I must explain that every mile I have travelled since leaving Colorado Springs has taken me farther and higher into the mountains. That afternoon I rode through lawn-like upland parks, with the great snow mass of Pike's Peak behind, and in front mountains bathed in rich atmospheric colouring of blue and violet, all very fine, but threatening to become monotonous, when the waggon road turned abruptly to the left, and crossed a broad, swift, mountain

river, the head-waters of the Platte.   There I found
the ranch to which I had been recommended, the
quarters of a great hunter named Link, which much
resembled a good country inn.   There was a pleasant,
friendly woman, but the men were all away, a thing
I always regret, as it gives me half an hour's work
at the horse before I can write to you.   I had hardly
come in when a very pleasant German lady, whom I
met at Manitou, with three gentlemen, arrived, and
we were as sociable as people could be.   We had a
splendid though rude supper.   While Mrs. Link was
serving us, and urging her good things upon us, she
was orating on the greediness of English people,
saying that "you would think they travelled through
the country only to gratify their palates;" and
addressed me, asking me if I had not observed it!
I am nearly always taken for a Dane or a Swede,
never for an Englishwoman, so I often hear a good
deal of outspoken criticism.   In the evening Mr.
Link returned, and there was a most vehement
discussion between him, an old hunter, a miner, and
the teamster who brought my pack, as to the route
by which I should ride through the mountains for
the next three or four days—because at that point I
was to leave the waggon road—and it was renewed
with increased violence the next morning, so that if
my nerves had not been of steel I should have been
appalled.   The old hunter acrimoniously said he

LETTER XI.

HALL'S GULCH, COLORADO, *November 6.*

IT was another cloudless morning, one of the many
here on which one awakes early, refreshed, and ready
to enjoy the fatigues of another day.   In our sunless,
misty climate you do not know the influence which
persistent fine weather exercises on the spirits. I have
been ten months in almost perpetual sunshine, and
now a single cloudy day makes me feel quite depressed. I did not leave till 9.30, because of the
slipperiness, and shortly after starting turned off
into the wilderness on a very dim trail. Soon seeing
a man riding a mile ahead, I rode on and overtook
him, and we rode eight miles together, which was
convenient to me, as without him I should several
times have lost the trail altogether. Then his fine
American horse, on which he had only ridden two
days, broke down, while my "mad, bad broncho," on
which I had been travelling for a fortnight, cantered

lightly over the snow. He was the only traveller I saw in a day of nearly twelve hours. I thoroughly enjoyed every minute of that ride. It concentrated all my faculties of admiration and of locality, for truly the track was a difficult one. I sometimes thought it deserved the bad name given to it at Link's. For the most part it keeps in sight of Tarryall Creek, one of the large affluents of the Platte, and is walled in on both sides by mountains, which are sometimes so close together as to leave only the narrowest canyon between them, at others breaking wide apart, till, after winding and climbing up and down for twenty-five miles, it lands one on a barren rock-girdled park, watered by a rapid fordable stream as broad as the Ouse at Huntingdon, snow-fed and ice-fringed, the park bordered by fantastic rocky hills, snow-covered and brightened only by a dwarf growth of the beautiful silver spruce. I have not seen anything hitherto so thoroughly wild and unlike the rest of these parts.

I rode up one great ascent where hills were tumbled about confusedly; and suddenly across the broad ravine, rising above the sunny grass and the deep-green pines, rose in glowing and shaded red against the glittering blue heaven a magnificent and unearthly range of mountains, as shapely as could be seen, rising into colossal points, cleft by deep blue ravines, broken up into sharks' teeth, with gigantic knobs and pinnacles rising from their inaccessible sides, very fair to

of him? or the son of man, that Thou visitest him?"
I rode up and down hills laboriously in snow-drifts,
getting off often to ease my faithful Birdie by walking
down ice-clad slopes, stopping constantly to feast my
eyes upon that changeless glory, always seeing some
new ravine, with its depths of colour or miraculous
brilliancy of red, or phantasy of form. Then below,
where the trail was locked into a deep canyon where
there was scarcely room for it and the river, there was
a beauty of another kind in solemn gloom. There
the stream curved and twisted marvellously, widening
into shallows, narrowing into deep boiling eddies, with
pyramidal firs and the beautiful silver spruce fringing
its banks, and often falling across it in artistic grace,
the gloom chill and deep, with only now and then a
light trickling through the pines upon the cold snow,
when suddenly turning round I saw behind, as if in
the glory of an eternal sunset, those flaming and fantastic peaks. The effect of the combination of winter
and summer was singular. The trail ran on the north
side the whole time, and the snow lay deep and pure
white, while not a wreath of it lay on the south side,
where abundant lawns basked in the warm sun.

The pitch pine, with its monotonous and somewhat rigid form, had disappeared; the white pine became scarce, both being displaced by the slim spires
and silvery green of the miniature silver spruce.
Valley and canyon were passed, the flaming ranges

were left behind, the upper altitudes became grim and mysterious.   I crossed a lake on the ice, and then came on a park surrounded by barren contorted hills, overtopped by snow mountains.   There, in some brushwood, we crossed a deepish stream on the ice, which gave way, and the fearful cold of the water stiffened my limbs for the rest of the ride.   All these streams become bigger as you draw nearer to their source, and shortly the trail disappeared in a broad rapid river, which we forded twice.   The trail was very difficult to recover.   It ascended ever in frost and snow, amidst scanty timber dwarfed by cold and twisted by storms, amidst solitudes such as one reads of in the High Alps ; there were no sounds to be heard but the crackle of ice and snow, the pitiful howling of wolves, and the hoot of owls.   The sun to me had long set ; the peaks which had blushed were pale and sad ; the twilight deepened into green ; but still " Excelsior !"   There were no happy homes with light of household fires ; above, the spectral mountains lifted their cold summits.   As darkness came on I began to fear that I had confused the cabin to which I had been directed with the rocks.   To confess the truth, I was cold, for my boots and stockings had frozen on my feet, and I was hungry too, having eaten nothing but raisins for fourteen hours.   After riding 30 miles I saw a light a little way from the track, and found it to be the cabin of the daughter of the

pleasant people with whom I had spent the previous
night. Her husband had gone to the plains, yet she,
with two infant children, was living there in perfect
security. Two pedlars, who were peddling their way
down from the mines, came in for a night's shelter
soon after I arrived — ill-looking fellows enough.
They admired Birdie in a suspicious fashion, and
offered to " swop " their pack-horse for her. I went
out the last thing at night and the first thing in the
morning to see that " the powny " was safe, for they
were very importunate on the subject of the " swop."
I had before been offered 150 dollars for her. I was
obliged to sleep with the mother and children, and
the pedlars occupied a room within ours. It was hot
and airless. The cabin was papered with the *Phreno-
logical Journal*, and in the morning I opened my eyes
on the very best portrait of Dr. Candlish I ever saw,
and grieved truly that I should never see that mass-
ive brow and fantastic face again.

Mrs. Link was an educated and very intelligent
young woman. The pedlars were Irish Yankees, and
the way in which they " traded " was as amusing as
" Sam Slick." They not only wanted to " swop " my
pony, but to " trade " my watch. They trade their
souls, I know. They displayed their wares for an
hour with much dexterous flattery and persuasive-
ness, but Mrs. Link was untemptable, and I was only
tempted into buying a handkerchief to keep the sun

off. There was another dispute about my route. It was the most critical day of my journey. If a snow-storm came on, I might be detained in the mountains for many weeks; but if I got through the snow and reached the Denver waggon-road, no detention would signify much. The pedlars insisted that I could not get through, for the road was not broken. Mrs. L. thought I could, and advised me to try, so I saddled Birdie and rode away.

More than half of the day was far from enjoyable. The morning was magnificent, but the light too dazzling, the sun too fierce. As soon as I got out I felt as if I should drop off the horse. My large handkerchief kept the sun from my neck, but the fierce heat caused soul and sense, brain and eye, to reel. I never saw or felt the like of it. I was at a height of 12,000 feet, where, of course, the air was highly rarefied, and the snow was so pure and dazzling that I was obliged to keep my eyes shut as much as possible to avoid snow blindness. The sky was a different and terribly fierce colour; and when I caught a glimpse of the sun, he was white and unwinking like a lime-ball light, yet threw off wicked scintillations. I suffered so from nausea, exhaustion, and pains from head to foot, that I felt as if I must lie down in the snow. It may have been partly the early stage of *soroche*, or mountain sickness. We plodded on for four hours, snow all round, and nothing else to be seen but an ocean of glistening peaks against that sky of infuriated blue. How I found my way I shall never know, for the only marks on the snow were occasional footprints of a man, and I had no means of knowing whether they led in the direction I ought to take. Earlier, before the snow became so deep, I passed the last great haunt of the magnificent mountain bison, but, unfortunately, saw nothing but horns and bones. Two months ago Mr. Link succeeded in separating a calf from the herd, and has partially domesticated it. It is a very ugly thing at seven months old, with a thick beard, and a short, thick, dark mane on its heavy shoulders. It makes a loud grunt like a pig. It can outrun their fastest horse, and it sometimes leaps over the high fence of the corral, and takes all the milk of five cows.

The snow grew seriously deep. Birdie fell thirty times, I am sure. She seemed unable to keep up at all, so I was obliged to get off and stumble along in her footmarks. By that time my spirit for overcoming difficulties had somewhat returned, for I saw a lie of country which I knew must contain South Park, and we had got under cover of a hill which kept off the sun. The trail had ceased; it was only one of those hunter's tracks which continually mislead one. The getting through the snow was awful work. I think we accomplished a mile in something over two hours. The snow was two feet

eight inches deep, and once we went down in a drift
the surface of which was rippled like sea sand,
Birdie up to her back, and I up to my shoulders!
At last we got through, and I beheld, with some sadness, the goal of my journey, "The Great Divide,"
the snowy range, and between me and it South Park,
a rolling prairie seventy-five miles long and over
10,000 feet high, treeless, bounded by mountains,
and so rich in sun-cured hay that one might fancy
that all the herds of Colorado could find pasture there.
Its chief centre is the rough mining town of Fairplay,
but there are rumours of great mineral wealth in
various quarters.   The region has been "rushed,"
and mining camps have risen at Alma and elsewhere,
so lawless and brutal that vigilance committees are
forming as a matter of necessity.   South Park is
closed, or nearly so, by snow during an ordinary
winter; and just now the great freight waggons are
carrying up the last supplies of the season, and taking
down women and other temporary inhabitants.   A
great many people come up here in the summer.   The
rarefied air produces great oppression on the lungs,
accompanied with bleeding.   It is said that you can
tell a new arrival by seeing him go about holding a
blood-stained handkerchief to his mouth.   But I
came down upon it from regions of ice and snow;
and as the snow which had fallen on it had all disappeared by evaporation and drifting, it looked to

me quite lowland and livable, though lonely and inde-
scribably mournful, "a silent sea," suggestive of "the
muffled oar." I cantered across the narrow end of
it, delighted to have got through the snow; and when
I struck the "Denver stage-road" I supposed that
all the difficulties of mountain travel were at an end,
but this has not turned out to be exactly the case.

A horseman shortly joined me and rode with me,
got me a fresh horse, and accompanied me for ten
miles. He was a picturesque figure and rode a very
good horse. He wore a big slouch hat, from under
which a number of fair curls hung nearly to his
waist. His beard was fair, his eyes blue, and his
complexion ruddy. There was nothing sinister in
his expression, and his manner was respectful and
frank. He was dressed in a hunter's buckskin suit
ornamented with beads, and wore a pair of exception-
ally big brass spurs. His saddle was very highly
ornamented. What was unusual was the number of
weapons he carried. Besides a rifle laid across his
saddle and a pair of pistols in the holsters, he carried
two revolvers and a knife in his belt, and a carbine
slung behind him. I found him what is termed
"good company." He told me a great deal about
the country and its wild animals, with some hunting
adventures, and a great deal about Indians and their
cruelty and treachery. All this time, having crossed
South Park, we were ascending the Continental

Divide by what I think is termed the Breckenridge Pass, on a fairly good waggon-road. We stopped at a cabin, where the woman seemed to know my companion, and, in addition to bread and milk, produced some venison steaks. We rode on again, and reached the crest of the Divide (see engraving), and saw snow-born streams starting within a quarter of a mile from each other, one for the Colorado and the Pacific, the other for the Platte and the Atlantic. Here I wished the hunter good-bye, and reluctantly turned north-east. It was not wise to go up the Divide at all, and it was necessary to do it in haste. On my way down I spoke to the woman at whose cabin I had dined, and she said, " I am sure you found Comanche Bill a real gentleman;" and I then knew that, if she gave me correct information, my intelligent, courteous companion was one of the most notorious desperadoes of the Rocky Mountains, and the greatest Indian exterminator on the frontier—a man whose father and family fell in a massacre at Spirit Lake by the hands of Indians, who carried away his sister, then a child of eleven. His life has since been mainly devoted to a search for this child, and to killing Indians wherever he can find them.

After riding twenty miles, which made the distance for that day fifty, I remounted Birdie to ride six miles farther, to a house which had been mentioned to me as a stopping-place. The road ascended to a height of 11,000 feet, and from thence I looked my last at the lonely, uplifted prairie sea. "Denver stage-road!" The worst, rudest, dismallest, darkest road I have yet travelled on, nothing but a winding ravine, the Platte canyon, pine-crowded and pine-darkened, walled in on both sides for six miles by pine-skirted mountains 12,000 feet high! Along this abyss for forty miles there are said to be only five houses, and were it not for miners going down, and freight-waggons going up, the solitude would be awful. As it was, I did not see a creature. It was four when I left South Park, and between those mountain walls and under the pines it soon became quite dark, a darkness which could be felt. The snow which had melted in the sun had refrozen, and was one sheet of smooth ice. Birdie slipped so alarmingly that I got off and walked, but then neither of us could keep our feet, and in the darkness she seemed so likely to fall upon me, that I took out of my pack the man's socks which had been given me at Perry's Park, and drew them on over her fore feet—an expedient which for a time succeeded admirably, and which I commend to all travellers similarly circumstanced. It was unutterably dark, and all these operations had to be performed by the sense of touch only. I remounted, allowed her to take her own way, as I could not see even her ears, and though her hind legs slipped badly, we contrived to get along through the narrowest part of the canyon, with a tumbling river close to the road. The pines were very dense, and sighed and creaked mournfully in the severe frost, and there were other *eerie* noises not easy to explain. At last, when the socks were nearly worn out, I saw the blaze of a camp fire, with two hunters sitting by it, on the hill-side, and at the mouth of a gulch something which looked like buildings. We got across the river partly on ice and partly by fording, and I found that this was the place where, in spite of its somewhat dubious reputation, I had been told that I could put up. A man came out in the sapient and good-natured stage of intoxication, and, the door being opened, I was confronted by a rough bar and a smoking, blazing kerosene lamp without a chimney. This is the worst place I have put up at as to food, lodging, and general character; an old and very dirty log-cabin, not chinked, with one dingy room used for cooking and feeding, in which a miner was lying very ill of fever; then a large roofless shed with a canvas side, which is to be an addition, and then the bar. They accounted for the disorder by the building operations. They asked me if I were the English lady written of in the *Denver News*, and for once I was glad that my fame had preceded me, as it seemed to secure me against being quietly " put out of the way." A horrible meal was served—dirty, greasy, disgusting.

A celebrated hunter, Bob Craik, came in to supper with a young man in tow, whom, in spite of his rough hunter's or miner's dress, I at once recognised as an English gentleman. It was their camp-fire which I had seen on the hill-side. This gentleman was lording it in true caricature fashion, with a Lord Dundreary drawl and a general execration of everything; while I sat in the chimney corner, speculating on the reason why many of the upper class of my countrymen —"High Toners," as they are called out here—make themselves so ludicrously absurd. They neither know how to hold their tongues or to carry their personal pretensions. An American is nationally assumptive, an Englishman personally so. He took no notice of me till something passed which showed him I was English, when his manner at once changed into courtesy, and his drawl was shortened by a half. He took pains to let me know that he was an officer in the Guards, of good family, on four months' leave, which he was spending in slaying buffalo and elk, and also that he had a profound contempt for everything American. I cannot think why Englishmen put on these broad, mouthing tones, and give so many personal details. They retired to their camp, and the landlord having passed into the sodden, sleepy stage of drunkenness, his wife asked if I should be afraid to sleep in the large canvas-sided, unceiled doorless shed, as they could not move the sick miner.

So I slept there on a shake-down, with the stars winking overhead through the roof, and the mercury showing 30° of frost.   I never told you that I once gave an unwary promise that I would not travel alone in Colorado unarmed, and that in consequence I left Estes Park with a Sharp's revolver loaded with ball-cartridge in my pocket, which has been the plague of my life.   Its bright ominous barrel peeped out in quiet Denver shops, children pulled it out to play with, or when my riding-dress hung up with it in the pocket, pulled the whole from the peg to the floor; and I cannot conceive of any circumstances in which I could feel it right to make any use of it, or in which it could do me any possible good.   Last night, however, I took it out, cleaned and oiled it, and laid it under my pillow, resolving to keep awake all night.   I slept as soon as I lay down, and never woke till the bright morning sun shone through the roof, making me ridicule my own fears and abjure pistols for ever!

                                              I. L. B.

LETTER XII.

DEER VALLEY, *November.*

TO-NIGHT I am in a beautiful place like a Dutch farm
—large, warm, bright, clean, with abundance of clean
food, and a clean, cold little bedroom to myself. But it
is very hard to write, for two free-tongued, noisy Irish-
women, who keep a miners' boarding-house in South
Park, and are going to winter quarters in a freight-
waggon, are telling the most fearful stories of violence,
vigilance committees, Lynch law, and "stringing," that
I ever heard. It turns one's blood cold only to think
that where I travel in perfect security, only a short
time ago men were being shot like skunks. At the
mining towns up above this nobody is thought anything of who has not killed a man—*i.e.* in a certain
set. These women had a boarder, only fifteen, who
thought he could not be anything till he had shot
somebody, and they gave an absurd account of the

lad dodging about with a revolver, and not getting up courage enough to insult any one, till at last he hid himself in the stable and shot the first Chinaman who entered. Things up there are just in that initial state which desperadoes love. A man accidentally shoves another in a saloon, or says a rough word at meals, and the challenge, "first finger on the trigger," warrants either in shooting the other at any subsequent time without the formality of a duel. Nearly all the shooting affrays arise from the most trivial causes in saloons and bar-rooms. The deeper quarrels, arising from jealousy or revenge, are few, and are usually about some woman not worth fighting for. At Alma and Fairplay vigilance committees have been lately formed, and when men act outrageously and make themselves generally obnoxious they receive a letter with a drawing of a tree, a man hanging from it, and a coffin below, on which is written "Fore-warned." They "git" in a few hours. When I said I spent last night at Hall's Gulch, there was quite a chorus of exclamations. My host there, they all said, would be "strung" before long. Did I know that a man was "strung" there yesterday? Had I not seen him hanging? He was on the big tree by the house, they said. Certainly, had I known what a ghastly burden that tree bore, I would have encountered the ice and gloom of the gulch rather than have slept there. They then told me a horrid tale of crime and

day after passing the teams except two men with a
" pack-jack." Birdie hates jacks, and rears and shies
as soon as she sees one. It was a bad road, one
shelving sheet of ice, and awfully lonely, and between
the peril of the mare breaking her leg on the ice and
that of being crushed by windfalls of timber, I had to
look out all day. Towards sunset I came to a cabin
where they " keep travellers," but the woman looked
so vinegar-faced that I preferred to ride four miles
farther, up a beautiful road winding along a sunny
gulch filled with silver spruce, bluer and more silvery
than any I have yet seen, and then crossed a divide,
from which the view in all the ecstasy of sunset
colour was perfectly glorious. It was enjoyment also
in itself to get out of the deep chasm in which I had
been immured all day. There is a train of twelve
freight-waggons here, each waggon with six horses,
but the teamsters carry their own camping blankets
and sleep either in their waggons or on the floor, so
the house is not crowded. It is a pleasant two-storey
log-house, not only chinked but lined with planed
timber. Each room has a great open chimney with
logs burning in it; there are pretty engravings on the
walls, and baskets full of creepers hanging from the
ceiling. This is the first settler's house I have been
in in which the ornamental has had any place.
There is a door to each room, the oak chairs are
bright with rubbing, and the floor, though unplaned,

is so clean that one might eat off it. The table is clean and abundant, and the mother and daughters, though they do all the work, look as trim as if they did none, and actually laugh heartily. The ranchman neither allows drink to be brought into the house nor to be drunk outside, and on this condition only he "keeps travellers." The freighters come in to supper quite well washed, and though twelve of them slept in the kitchen, by nine o'clock there was not a sound. This freighting business is most profitable. I think that the charge is three cents per pound from Denver to South Park, and there much of the freight is transferred to "pack-jacks" and carried up to the mines. A railroad, however, is contemplated. I breakfasted with the family after the freight train left, and instead of sitting down to gobble up the remains of a meal, they had a fresh tablecloth and hot food. The buckets are all polished oak, with polished brass bands; the kitchen utensils are bright as rubbing can make them; and, more wonderful still, the girls black their boots. Blacking usually is an unused luxury, and frequently is not kept in houses. My boots have only been blacked once during the last two months.

DENVER, *November 9.*

I could not make out whether the superiority of the Deer Valley settlers extended beyond material things, but a teamster I met in the evening said it "made him

more of a man to spend a night in such a house." In
Colorado whisky is significant of all evil and violence,
and is the cause of most of the shooting affrays in the
mining camps. There are few moderate drinkers; it
is seldom taken except to excess. The great local
question in the Territory, and just now the great
electoral issue, is drink or no drink, and some of the
papers are openly advocating a prohibitive liquor law.
Some of the districts, such as Greeley, in which liquor
is prohibited, are without crime, and in several of the
stock-raising and agricultural regions through which
I have travelled, where it is practically excluded, the
doors are never locked, and the miners leave their
silver bricks in their waggons unprotected at night.
People say that on coming from the Eastern States
they hardly realise at first the security in which they
live. There is no danger and no fear. But the truth
of the proverbial saying, " There is no God west of the
Missouri," is everywhere manifest. The " almighty
dollar " is the true divinity, and its worship is universal. " Smartness " is the quality thought most of.
The boy who " gets on " by cheating at his lessons is
praised for being a " smart boy," and his satisfied
parents foretell that he will make a " smart man." A
man who overreaches his neighbour, but who does it
so cleverly that the law cannot take hold of him, wins
an envied reputation as a " smart man," and stories of
this species of smartness are told admiringly round

brown plains to Denver.   Not a tree or shrub was to
be seen, everything was rioting in summer heat and
drought, while behind lay the last grand canyon of
the mountains, dark with pines and cool with snow.
I left the track and took a short cut over the prairie
to Denver, passing through an encampment of the
Ute Indians about 500 strong, a disorderly and dirty
huddle of lodges, ponies, men, squaws, children, skins,
bones, and raw meat.

The Americans will never solve the Indian pro-
blem till the Indian is extinct. They have treated
them after a fashion which has intensified their
treachery and "devilry" as enemies, and as friends
reduces them to a degraded pauperism, devoid of the
very first elements of civilisation. The only difference
between the savage and the civilised Indian is that
the latter carries firearms and gets drunk on whisky.
The Indian Agency has been a sink of fraud and corruption; it is said that barely thirty per cent of the
allowance ever reaches those for whom it is voted; and
the complaints of shoddy blankets, damaged flour, and
worthless firearms are universal.   "To get rid of the
Injuns" is the phrase used everywhere.   Even their
"reservations" do not escape seizure practically ;
for if gold "breaks out" on them they are "rushed,"
and their possessors are either compelled to accept
land farther west or are shot off and driven off.   One
of the surest agents in their destruction is vitriolised

whisky.   An attempt has recently been made to
cleanse the Augean stable of the Indian Department,
but it has met with signal failure, the usual result in
America of every effort to purify the official atmosphere.   Americans specially love superlatives.   The
phrases "biggest in the world," "finest in the world,"
are on all lips.   Unless the President is a strong man
they will soon come to boast that their government is
composed of the "biggest scoundrels" in the world.

As I rode into Denver and away from the mountains the view became glorious, as range above range
crowned with snow came into sight.   I was sure that
three glistening peaks seventy miles north were the
peerless shapeliness of Long's Peak, the king of the
Rocky Mountains, and the "mountain fever" returned
so severely that I grudged every hour spent on the
dry, hot plains.   The range looked lovelier and
sublimer than when I first saw it from Greeley, all
spiritualised in the wonderful atmosphere.   I went
direct to Evans's house, where I found a hearty welcome, as they had been anxious about my safety, and
Evans almost at once arrived from Estes Park with
three elk, one grizzly, and one bighorn in his waggon.
Regarding a place and life one likes (in spite of all
lessons) one is sure to think, "To-morrow shall be as
this day, and much more abundant;" and all through
my tour I had thought of returning to Estes Park
and finding everything just as it was.   Evans brought

the unwelcome news that the goodly fellowship was broken up. The Dewys and Mr. Waller were in Denver, and the house was dismantled, Mr. and Mrs. Edwards alone remaining, who were, however, expecting me back. Saturday, though like a blazing summer day, was wonderful in its beauty, and after sunset the afterglow was richer and redder than I have ever seen it, but the heavy crimson betokened severe heat, which came on yesterday, and was hardly bearable. I attended service twice at the Episcopal Church, where the service was beautifully read and sung; but in a city in which men preponderate the congregation was mainly composed of women, who fluttered their fans in a truly distracting way. Except for the churchgoing there were few perceptible signs of Sunday in Denver, which was full of rowdies from the mountain mining camps. You can hardly imagine the delight of joining in those grand old prayers after so long a deprivation. The "Te Deum" sounded heavenly in its magnificence; but the heat was so tremendous that it was hard to "warstle" through the day. They say that they have similar outbreaks of solar fury all through the winter.

GOLDEN CITY, *November 13.*

Pleasant as Denver was, with the Dewys and so many kind friends there, it was too much of the "wearing world" either for my health or taste, and

I left for my sixteen miles' ride to this place at four on Monday afternoon with the sun still hot. Passing by a bare, desolate-looking cemetery, I asked a sad-looking woman who was leaning on the gate if she could direct me to Golden City. I repeated the question twice before I got an answer, and then, though easily to be accounted for, it was wide of the mark. In most doleful tones she said, " Oh, go to the minister; I might tell you, may be, but it's too great a responsibility ; go to the ministers, they can tell you ! " And she returned to her tears for some one whose spirit she was doubtless thinking of as in the Golden City of our hopes. That sixteen miles seemed like one mile, after sunset, in the rapturous freshness of the Colorado air, and Birdie, after her two days' rest and with a lightened load, galloped across the prairie as if she enjoyed it. I did not reach this gorge till late, and it was an hour after dark before I groped my way into this dark, unlighted mining town, where, however, we were most fortunate both as to stable and accommodation for myself.

BOULDER, *November 16.*

I fear you will grow tired of the details of these journal letters. To a person sitting quietly at home, Rocky Mountain travelling, like Rocky Mountain scenery, must seem very monotonous ; but not so to me, to whom the pure, dry mountain air

is the elixir of life. At Golden City I parted
for a time from my faithful pony, as Clear Creek
Canyon, which leads from it to Idaho, is entirely
monopolised by a narrow-gauge railroad, and is inaccessible for horses or mules. To be without a
horse in these mountains is to be reduced to complete
helplessness. My great wish was to see Green Lake,
situated near the timber line above Georgetown (said
to be the highest town in the United States), at a
height of 9000 feet. A single day took me from the
heat of summer into the intense cold of winter.
Golden City by daylight showed its meanness and
belied its name. It is ungraded, with here and there
a piece of wooden sidewalk, supported on posts, up
to which you ascend by planks. Brick, pine, and
log houses are huddled together, every other house is
a saloon, and hardly a woman is to be seen. My
landlady apologised for the very exquisite little bedroom which she gave me by saying "it was not quite
as she would like it, but she had never had a lady in
her house before." The young "lady" who waited
at breakfast said, "I've been thinking about you, and
I'm certain sure you're an authoress." The day, as
usual, was glorious. Think of November half through
and scarcely even a cloud in the sky, except the
vermilion cloudlets which accompany the sun at his
rising and setting! They say that winter never "sets
in" there in the Foot Hills, but that there are spells

of cold, alternating with bright, hot weather, and that
the snow never lies on the ground so as to interfere
with the feed of cattle. Golden City rang with oaths
and curses, especially at the depôt. Americans are
given over to the most atrocious swearing, and the
blasphemous use of our Saviour's name is peculiarly
revolting. Golden City stands at the mouth of
Toughcuss, otherwise Clear Creek Canyon, which
many people think the grandest scenery in the
mountains, as it twists and turns marvellously, and
its stupendous sides are nearly perpendicular, while
farther progress is to all appearance continually
blocked by great masses of rock and piles of snow-
covered mountains. Unfortunately, its sides have
been almost entirely denuded of timber, mining
operations consuming any quantity of it. The
narrow-gauge, steep-grade railway, which runs up the
canyon for the convenience of the rich mining districts of Georgetown, Black Hawk, and Central City,
is a curiosity of engineering. The track has partly
been blasted out of the sides of the canyon, and has
partly been " built " by making a bed of stones in the
creek itself, and laying the track across them. I have
never seen such churlishness and incivility as in the
officials of that railroad and the stage-lines which
connect with it, or met with such preposterous
charges. They have handsome little cars on the
route, but though the passengers paid full fare, they

put us into a baggage-car because the season was over, and in order to see anything I was obliged to sit on the floor at the door. The singular grandeur cannot be described. It is a mere gash cut by the torrent, twisted, walled, chasmed, weather-stained, with the most brilliant colouring, generally dark with shadow, but its utter desolation occasionally revealed by a beam of intense sunshine. A few stunted pines and cedars, spared because of their inaccessibility, hung here and there out of the rifts. Sometimes the walls of the abyss seemed to meet overhead, and then widening out, the rocks assumed fantastic forms, all grandeur, sublimity, and almost terror. After two hours of this, the track came to an end, and the canyon widened sufficiently for a road, all stones, holes, and sidings. There a great " Concord coach " waited for us, intended for twenty passengers, and a mountain of luggage in addition, and the four passengers without any luggage sat on the seat behind the driver, so that the huge thing bounced and swung upon the straps on which it was hung so as to recall the worst horrors of New Zealand staging. The driver never spoke without an oath, and though two ladies were passengers, cursed his splendid horses the whole time. Formerly, even the most profane men intermitted their profanity in the presence of women, but they " have changed all that." Every one I saw up there seemed in a bad temper. I suspect that

next day, and much feared that I should lose Green Lake, the goal of my journey. We drove through the narrow, piled-up, irregular street, crowded with miners standing in groups, or drinking and gaming under the verandahs, to a good hotel declivitously situated, where I at once inquired if I could get to Green Lake. The landlord said he thought not; the snow was very deep, and no one had been up for five weeks, but for my satisfaction he would send to a stable and inquire. The amusing answer came back, "If it's the English lady travelling in the mountains, she can have a horse, but not any one else."

I. L. B.

LETTER XIII.

The Blight of Mining—Green Lake—Golden City—Benighted—
    Vertigo—Boulder Canyon—Financial straits—A hard Ride—
    The last Cent—A Bachelor's Home—Mountain Jim—A Sur-
    prise—A Night Arrival—Making the best of it—Scanty
    Fare.

BOULDER, *November.*

THE answer regarding a horse (at the end of my former
letter) was given to the landlord outside the hotel, and
presently he came in and asked my name, and if I were
the lady who had crossed from Link's to South Park by
Tarryall Creek; so news travels fast.   In five minutes
the horse was at the door, with a clumsy two-horned
side-saddle, and I started at once for the upper regions.
It was an exciting ride, much spiced with apprehen-
sion.   The evening shadows had darkened over
Georgetown, and I had 2000 feet to climb, or give up
Green Lake.   I shall forget many things, but never
the awfulness and hugeness of that scenery.   I went
up a steep track by Clear Creek, then a succession
of frozen waterfalls in a widened and then narrowed
valley, whose frozen sides looked 5000 feet high.
That is the region of enormous mineral wealth in

silver. There are the "Terrible" and other mines, whose shares you can see quoted daily in the share lists in the *Times*, sometimes at cent per cent premium, and then down to 25 discount. These mines, with their prolonged subterranean workings, their stamping and crushing mills, and the smelting works which have been established near them, fill the district with noise, hubbub, and smoke by night and day; but I had turned altogether aside from them into a still region, where each miner in solitude was grubbing for himself, and confiding to none his finds or disappointments. Agriculture restores and beautifies, mining destroys and devastates; turning the earth inside out, making it hideous, and blighting every green thing, as it usually blights man's heart and soul. There was mining everywhere along that grand road, with all its destruction and devastation, its digging, burrowing, gulching, and sluicing; and up all along the seemingly inaccessible heights were holes with their roofs log-supported, in which solitary and patient men were selling their lives for treasure. Down by the stream, all among the icicles, men were sluicing and washing, and everywhere along the heights were the scars of hardly-passable trails, too steep even for pack-jacks, leading to the holes, and down which the miner packs the ore on his back. Many a heart has been broken for the few finds which have been made along those hill-sides.

It was something to reach that height and see the far-off glory of the sunset, and by it to be reminded that neither God nor His sun had yet deserted the world. But the sun was fast going down, and even as I gazed upon the wonderful vision the glory vanished, and the peaks became sad and gray. It was strange to be the only human being at that glacial altitude, and to descend again through a foot of untrodden snow and over sloping sheets of ice into the darkness, and to see the hill-sides like a firmament of stars, each showing the place where a solitary man in his hole was delving for silver. The view, as long as I could see it, was quite awful. It looked as if one could not reach Georgetown without tumbling down a precipice. Precipices there were in plenty along the road, skirted with ice to their verge. It was the only ride which required nerve that I have taken in Colorado, and it was long after dark when I returned from my exploit.

I left Georgetown at eight the next morning on the Idaho stage, in glorious cold. In this dry air it is quite warm if there are only a few degrees of frost. The sun does not rise in Georgetown till eleven now; I doubt if it rises there at all in the winter! After four hours' fearful bouncing, the baggage-car again received us, but this time the conductor, remarking that he supposed I was just travelling to see the country, gave me his chair and put it on the plat-

form, so that I had an excellent view of that truly
sublime canyon. For economy I dined in a restaurant
in Golden City, and at three remounted my trusty
Birdie, intending to arrive here that night. The adventure I met with is almost too silly to tell. When
I left Golden City it was a brilliant summer afternoon, and not too hot. They could not give any
directions at the stable, and told me to go out on the
Denver track till I met some one who could direct
me, which started me off wrong from the first. After
riding about two miles I met a man who told me I
was all wrong, and directed me across the prairie till
I met another, who gave me so many directions that
I forgot them, and was irretrievably lost. The afterglow, seen to perfection on the open plain, was wonderful. Just as it grew dark I rode after a teamster
who said I was then four miles farther from Boulder
than when I left Golden, and directed me to a house
seven miles off. I suppose he thought I should
know, for he told me to cross the prairie till I came
to a place where three tracks are seen, and there to
take the best-travelled one, steering all the time by
the north star. His directions did bring me to tracks,
but it was then so dark that I could see nothing,
and soon became so dark that I could not even see
Birdie's ears, and was lost and benighted. I rode on,
hour after hour, in the darkness and solitude, the
prairie all round and a firmament of frosty stars

overhead. The prairie wolf howled now and then, and occasionally the lowing of cattle gave me hope of human proximity. But there was nothing but the lone wild plain. You can hardly imagine the longing to see a light, to hear a voice, the intensely eerie feeling of being alone in that vast solitude. It was freezing very sharply and was very cold, and I was making up my mind to steer all night for the Pole Star, much fearing that I should be brought up by one of the affluents of the Platte, or that Birdie would tire, when I heard the undertoned bellowing of a bull, which, from the snorting and rooting up of earth, seemed to be disputing the right of way, and the pony was afraid to pass. While she was scuffling about, I heard a dog bark and a man swear; then I saw a light, and in another minute found myself at a large house, where I knew the people, only eleven miles from Denver! It was nearly midnight, and light, warmth, and a good bed were truly welcome.

You can form no idea of what the glory on the plains is just before sunrise. Like the afterglow, for a great height above the horizon there is a shaded band of the most intense and glowing orange, while the mountains which reflect the yet unrisen sun have the purple light of amethysts. I left early, but soon lost the track and was lost; but knowing that a sublime gash in the mountains was Bear Canyon, quite near Boulder, I struck across the prairie for it, and then found the Boulder track. "The best-laid schemes of men and mice gang aft agee," and my exploits came to an untimely end to-day. On arriving here, instead of going into the mountains, I was obliged to go to bed in consequence of vertigo, headache, and faintness, produced by the intense heat of the sun. In all that weary land there was no "shadow of a great rock" under which to rest. The gravelly, baked soil reflected the fiery sun, and it was nearly maddening to look up at the cool blue of the mountains, with their stretches of pines and their deep indigo shadows. Boulder is a hideous collection of frame houses on the burning plain, but it aspires to be a "city" in virtue of being a "distributing point" for the settlements up the Boulder Canyon, and of the discovery of a coal-seam.

LONGMOUNT, *November.*

I got up very early this morning, and on a hired horse went nine miles up the Boulder Canyon, which is much extolled, but I was greatly disappointed with everything except its superb waggon-road, and much disgusted with the laziness of the horse. A ride of fifteen miles across the prairie brought me here early in the afternoon, but of the budget of letters which I expected there is not one. Birdie looks in such capital condition that

my host here can hardly believe that she has travelled over 500 miles. I am feeling " the pinch of
poverty" rather severely. When I have paid my
bill here I shall have exactly twenty-six cents left.
Evans was quite unable to pay the hundred dollars
which he owes me, and, to save themselves, the
Denver banks, though they remain open, have suspended payment, and would not cash my circular
notes. The financial straits are very serious, and
the unreasoning panic which has set in makes them
worse.   The present state of matters is—nobody
has any money, so nothing is worth anything. The
result to me is that, *nolens volens*, I must go up to
Estes Park, where I can live without ready money,
and remain there till things change for the better.
It does not seem a very hard fate! Long's Peak
rises in purple gloom, and I long for the cool air
and unfettered life of the solitary blue hollow at its
base.

ESTES PARK, *November 20.*

Would that three notes of admiration were all I need
give to my grand solitary, uplifted, sublime, remote,
beast-haunted lair, which seems more indescribable
than ever; but you will wish to know how I have sped,
and I wish you to know my present singular circumstances. I left Longmount at eight on Saturday morning,
rather heavily loaded, for in addition to my own luggage I was asked to carry the mail-bag, which was heavy

with newspapers. Edwards, with his wife and family, were still believed to be here. A heavy snowstorm was expected, and all the sky—that vast dome which spans the plains—was overcast; but over the mountains it was a deep, still, sad blue, into which snowy peaks rose sunlighted. It was a lonely, mournful-looking morning, but when I reached the beautiful canyon of the St. Vrain, the sad blue became brilliant, and the sun warm and scintillating. Ah, how beautiful and incomparable the ride up here is, infinitely more beautiful than the much-vaunted parts I have seen elsewhere. There is, first, this beautiful hill-girdled valley of fair savannahs, through which the bright St. Vrain curves in and out amidst a tangle of cotton-wood and withered clematis and Virginia creeper, which two months ago made the valley gay with their scarlet and gold. Then the canyon, with its fantastically-stained walls; then the long ascent through sweeping foothills to the gates of rock at a height of 9000 feet; then the wildest and most wonderful scenery for twenty miles, in which you cross thirteen ranges from 9000 to 11,000 feet high, pass through countless canyons and gulches, cross thirteen dark fords, and finally descend, through M'Ginn's Gulch, upon this, the gem of the Rocky Mountains. It was a weird ride. I got on very slowly. The road is a hard one for any horse, specially for a heavily-loaded one, and at the end of several weeks

of severe travel.   When I had ridden fifteen miles I
stopped at the ranch where people usually get food,
but it was empty, and the next was also deserted.
So I was compelled to go to the last house, where two
young men are "baching."   There I had to decide
between getting a meal for myself or a feed for the
pony; but the young man, on hearing of my sore
poverty, trusted me "till next time."   His house,
for order and neatness, and a sort of sprightliness of
cleanliness—the comfort of cleanliness without its
severity—is a pattern to all women, while the clear
eyes and manly self-respect which the habit of total
abstinence gives in this country are a pattern to all
men.   He cooked me a splendid dinner, with good
tea.   After dinner I opened the mail-bag, and was
delighted to find an accumulation of letters from you;
but I sat much too long there, forgetting that I had
twenty miles to ride, which could hardly be done in
less than six hours.   It was then brilliant.   I had
not realised the magnificence of that ride when I took
it before, but the pony was tired, and I could not
hurry her, and the distance seemed interminable, as
after every range I crossed another range.   Then
came a region of deep, dark, densely-wooded gulches,
only a few feet wide, and many fords, and from their
cold depths I saw the last sunlight fade from the
brows of precipices 4000 feet high.   It was eerie, as
darkness came on, to wind in and out in the pine-

was loaded.   The desperado was heartily glad to see me, and sending the man and fur-laden horse on to his cabin, he turned with me to Evans's; and as the cold was very severe, and Birdie was very tired, we dismounted and walked the remaining three miles. All my visions of a comfortable reception and good meal after my long ride vanished with his first words. The Edwardses had left for the winter on the previous morning, but had not passed through Longmount; the cabin was dismantled, the stores were low, and two young men, Mr. Kavan, a miner, and Mr. Buchan, whom I was slightly acquainted with before, were "baching" there to look after the stock until Evans, who was daily expected, returned.   The other settler and his wife had left the Park, so there was not a woman within twenty-five miles.   A fierce wind had arisen, and the cold was awful, which seemed to make matters darker.   I did not care in the least about myself, I could rough it, and enjoy doing so, but I was very sorry for the young men, who, I knew, would be much embarrassed by the sudden appearance of a lady for an indefinite time.   But the difficulty had to be faced, and I walked in and took them by surprise as they were sitting smoking by the fire in the living-room, which was dismantled, unswept, and wretched-looking.   The young men did not show any annoyance, but exerted themselves to prepare a meal, and courteously made Jim share it.   After he

had gone, I boldly confessed my impecunious circumstances, and told them that I must stay there till
things changed, that I hoped not to inconvenience
them in any way, and that by dividing the work
among us they would be free to be out hunting. So
we agreed to make the best of it. [Our arrangements,
which we supposed would last only two or three days,
extended over nearly a month. Nothing could exceed
the courtesy and good feeling which these young men
showed. It was a very pleasant time on the whole,
and when we separated they told me that though they
were much "taken aback" at first, they felt at last
that we could get on in the same way for a year, in
which I cordially agreed.] Sundry practical difficulties had to be faced and overcome. There was one
of the common spring mattresses of the country in
the little room which opened from the living-room,
but nothing upon it. This was remedied by making
a large bag and filling it with hay. Then there were
neither sheets, towels, nor table-cloths. This was
irremediable, and I never missed the first or last.
Candles were another loss, and we had only one
paraffin lamp. I slept all night in spite of a gale
which blew all Sunday and into Monday afternoon,
threatening to lift the cabin from the ground, and
actually removing part of the roof from the little
room between the kitchen and living-room, in which
we used to dine. Sunday was brilliant, but nearly a

hurricane, and I dared not stir outside the cabin. The parlour was two inches deep in the mud from the roof. We nominally divide the cooking. Mr. Kavan makes the best bread I ever ate; they bring in wood and water, and wash the supper-things, and I "do" my room and the parlour, wash the breakfast-things, and a number of etceteras. My room is easily "done," but the parlour is a never-ending business. I have swept shovelfuls of mud out of it three times to-day. There is nothing to dust it with but a buffalo's tail, and every now and then a gust descends the open chimney and drives the wood ashes all over the room. However, I have found an old shawl which answers for a table-cloth, and have made our "parlour" look a little more habitable. Jim came in yesterday in a silent mood, and sat looking vacantly into the fire. The young men said that this mood was the usual precursor of an "ugly fit."

Food is a great difficulty. Of thirty milch cows only one is left, and she does not give milk enough for us to drink. The only meat is some pickled pork, very salt and hard, which I cannot eat, and the hens lay less than one egg a day. Yesterday morning I made some rolls, and made the last bread into a bread-and-butter pudding, which we all enjoyed. To-day I found part of a leg of beef hanging in the waggon-shed, and we were elated with the prospect of fresh meat, but on cutting into it we found it green

LETTER XIV.

A dismal Ride — A Desperado's Tale — "Lost! Lost! Lost!"—
Winter Glories—Solitude—Hard Times—Intense Cold—A
Pack of Wolves—The Beaver Dams—Ghostly Scenes—Venison
Steaks—Our Evenings.

ESTES PARK.

I MUST attempt to put down the trifling events of
each day just as they occur. The second time that
I was left alone Mr. Nugent came in looking very
black, and asked me to ride with him to see the
beaver dams on the Black Canyon. No more whist-
ling or singing, or talking to his beautiful mare, or
sparkling repartee. His mood was as dark as the
sky overhead, which was black with an impending
snowstorm. He was quite silent, struck his horse
often, started off on a furious gallop, and then throwing his mare on her haunches close to me, said,
"You're the first man or woman who's treated me
like a human being for many a year." So he said in
this dark mood, but Mr. and Mrs. Dewy, who took a
very deep interest in his welfare, always treated him
as a rational, intelligent gentleman, and in his better
moments he spoke of them with the warmest appreciation. "If you want to know," he continued,

"how nearly a man can become a devil, I'll tell you now." There was no choice, and we rode up the canyon, and I listened to one of the darkest tales of ruin I have ever heard or read. Its early features were very simple. His father was a British officer quartered at Montreal, of a good old Irish family. From his account he was an ungovernable boy, imperfectly educated, and tyrannising over a loving but weak mother. When seventeen years old he saw a young girl at church whose appearance he described as being of angelic beauty, and fell in love with her with all the intensity of an uncontrolled nature. He saw her three times, but scarcely spoke to her. On his mother opposing his wish and treating it as a boyish folly, he took to drink " to spite her," and almost as soon as he was eighteen, maddened by the girl's death, he ran away from home, entered the service of the Hudson's Bay Company, and remained in it for several years, only leaving it because he found even that lawless life too strict for him. Then, being as I suppose about twenty-seven, he entered the service of the United States Government, and became one of the famous Indian Scouts of the Plains, distinguishing himself by some of the most daring deeds on record, and some of the bloodiest crimes. Some of these tales I have heard before, but never so terribly told. Years must have passed in that service, till he became a character known through all the West, and much dreaded for his readiness to take offence, and his equal readiness with his revolver. Vain, even in his dark mood, he told me that he was idolised by women, and that in his worst hours he was always chivalrous to good women. He described himself as riding through camps in his scout's dress with a red scarf round his waist, and sixteen golden curls, eighteen inches long, hanging over his shoulders. The handsome, even superbly handsome, side of his face was towards me as he spoke. As a scout and as an armed escort of emigrant parties he was evidently implicated in all the blood and broil of a lawless region and period, and went from bad to worse, varying his life by drunken sprees, which brought nothing but violence and loss. The narrative seemed to lack some link, for I next found him on a homestead in Missouri, from whence he came to Colorado a few years ago. There, again, something was dropped out, but I suspect, and not without reason, that he joined one or more of those gangs of "border ruffians" which for so long raided through Kansas, perpetrating such massacres and outrages as that of the Marais du Cygne. His fame for violence and ruffianism preceded him into Colorado, where his knowledge of and love of the mountains have earned him the *sobriquet* he now bears. He has a squatter's claim and forty head of cattle, and is a successful trapper besides, but envy and vindictiveness are raging within him. He

gets money, goes to Denver, and spends large sums in
the maddest dissipation, making himself a terror, and
going beyond even such desperadoes as "Texas Jack"
and "Wild Bill;" and when the money is done
returns to his mountain den, full of hatred and self-
scorn, till the next time. Of course I cannot give
details. The story took three hours to tell, and was
crowded with terrific illustrations of a desperado's
career, told with a rush of wild eloquence that was
truly thrilling. When the snow, which for some time
had been falling, compelled him to break off and
guide me to a sheltered place from which I could
make my own way back again, he stopped his horse
and said, " Now you see a man who has made a devil
of himself! Lost! Lost! Lost! I believe in God.
I've given Him no choice but to put me with ' the
devil and his angels.' I'm afraid to die. You've
stirred the better nature in me too late. I can't
change. If ever a man were a slave, I am. Don't
speak to me of repentance and reformation. I can't
reform. Your voice reminded me of ——." Then
in feverish tones, "How dare you ride with me?
You won't speak to me again, will you?" He made
me promise to keep one or two things secret whether
he were living or dead, and I promised, for I had no
choice; but they come between me and the sunshine
sometimes, and I wake at night to think of them. I
wish I had been spared the regret and excitement of

that afternoon. A less ungovernable nature would never have spoken as he did, nor told me what he did ; but his proud, fierce soul all poured itself out then, with hatred and self-loathing, blood on his hands and murder in his heart, though even then he could not be altogether other than a gentleman, or altogether divest himself of fascination, even when so tempestuously revealing the darkest points of his character. My soul dissolved in pity for his dark, lost, self-ruined life, as he left me and turned away in the blinding storm to the Snowy Range, where he said he was going to camp out for a fortnight; a man of great abilities, real genius, singular gifts, and with all the chances in life which other men have had. How far more terrible than the " *Actum est : periisti*" of Cowper is his exclamation, " Lost ! Lost ! Lost ! "

The storm was very severe, and the landmarks being blotted out, I lost my way in the snow, and when I reached the cabin after dark I found it still empty, for the two hunters, on returning, finding that I had gone out, had gone in search of me. The snow cleared off late, and intense frost set in. My room is nearly the open air, being built of unchinked logs, and, as in the open air, one requires to sleep with the head buried in blankets, or the eyelids and breath freeze. The sunshine has been brilliant to-day. I took a most beautiful ride to Black Canyon to look for the horses. Every day some new beauty, or effect

of snow and light, is to be seen.   Nothing that I have
seen in Colorado compares with Estes Park; and now
that the weather is magnificent, and the mountain
tops above the pine woods are pure white, there is
nothing of beauty or grandeur for which the heart can
wish that is not here; and it is health-giving, with
pure air, pure water, and absolute dryness.   But there
is something very solemn, at times almost overwhelming, in the winter solitude.   I have never
experienced anything like it even when I lived on
the slopes of Hualalai.   When the men are out
hunting I know not where, or at night, when storms
sweep down from Long's Peak, and the air is full of
stinging, tempest-driven snow, and there is barely a
probability of any one coming, or of any communi-
cation with the world at all, then the stupendous
mountain ranges which lie between us and the plains
grow in height till they become impassable barriers,
and the bridgeless rivers grow in depth, and I wonder
if all my life is to be spent here in washing and
sweeping and baking.   To-day has been one of
manual labour.   We did not breakfast till 9.30, then
the men went out, and I never sat down till two.   I
cleaned the living-room and the kitchen, swept a path
through the rubbish in the passage-room, washed up,
made and baked a batch of rolls and four pounds of
sweet biscuits, cleaned some tins and pans, washed
some clothes, and gave things generally a "redding

up." There is a little thick buttermilk, fully six weeks old, at the bottom of a churn, which I use for raising the rolls; but Mr. Kavan, who makes "lovely" bread, puts some flour and water to turn sour near the stove, and this succeeds admirably. I also made a most unsatisfactory investigation into the state of my apparel. I came to Colorado now nearly three months ago, with a small carpet - bag containing clothes, none of them new; and these, by legitimate wear, the depredations of calves, and the necessity of tearing some of them up for dish-cloths, are reduced to a single change! I have a solitary pocket-hand-kerchief and one pair of stockings, such a mass of darns that hardly a trace of the original wool remains. Owing to my inability to get money in Denver I am almost without shoes, have nothing but a pair of slippers and some "arctics." For outer garments— well, I have a trained black silk dress, with a black silk polonaise! and nothing else but my old flannel riding-suit, which is quite threadbare, and requires such frequent mending that I am sometimes obliged to "dress" for supper, and patch and darn it during the evening. You will laugh, but it is singular that one can face the bitter winds with the mercury at zero and below it, in exactly the same clothing which I wore in the tropics! It is only the extreme dry-ness of the air which renders it possible to live in such clothing. We have arranged the work

cowardly, I believe. This morning was black with clouds, and a snowstorm was threatened, and about 700 cattle and a number of horses came in long files from the valleys and canyons where they maraud, their instinct teaching them to seek the open and the protection of man. I was alone in the cabin this afternoon when Mr. Nugent, whom we believed to be on the Snowy Range, walked in very pale and haggard-looking, and coughing severely. He offered to show me the trail up one of the grandest of the canyons, and I could not refuse to go. The Fall river has had its source completely altered by the operations of the beavers. Their engineering skill is wonderful. In one place they have made a lake by damming up the stream; in another their works have created an island, and they have made several falls. Their storehouses, of course, are carefully concealed. By this time they are about full for the winter. We saw quantities of young cotton-wood and aspen-trees, with stems about as thick as my arm, lying where these industrious creatures have felled them ready for their use. They always work at night and in concert. Their long, sharp teeth are used for gnawing down the trees, but their mason-work is done entirely with their flat, trowel-like tails. In its natural state the fur is very durable, and is as full of long black hairs as that of the sable, but as sold, all these hairs have been plucked out of it. The canyon was gloria very depressing effect, and all the scenery appears in its grimness of black and gray. We have lost three horses, including Birdie, and have nothing to entice them with, and not an animal to go and drive them in with. I put my great mare in the corral myself, and Mr. Kavan put his in afterwards and secured the bars, but the wolves were holding a carnival again last night, and we think that the horses were scared and stampeded, as otherwise they would not have leaped the fence. The men are losing their whole day in looking for them. On their return they said that they had seen Mr. Nugent returning to his cabin by the other side and the lower ford of the Thompson, and that he had "an awfully ugly fit on him," so that they were glad that he did not come near us. The evening is setting in sublime in its blackness. Late in the afternoon I caught a horse which was snuffing at the sheaf oats, and had a splendid gallop on the Longmount trail with the two great hunting dogs. In returning, in the grimness of the coming storm, I had that view of the Park which I saw first in the glories of an autumn sunset. Life was all dead; the dragon-flies no longer darted in the sunshine, the cotton-woods had shed their last amber leaves, the crimson trailers of the wild vines were bare, the stream itself had ceased its tinkle and was numb in fetters of ice, a few withered flower-stalks only told of the brief bright glory of the summer. The Park

can fancy my surprise, on going into the kitchen, to find a dish of smoking steaks of venison on the table. We ate like famished people, and enjoyed our meal thoroughly. Just before I came the young men had shot an elk, which they intended to sell in Denver, and the grand carcass, with great branching antlers, hung outside the shed. Often while vainly trying to swallow some pickled pork I had looked across to the tantalising animal, but it was not to be thought of. However, this morning, as the young men felt the pinch of hunger even more than I did, and the prospects of packing it to Denver became worse, they decided on cutting into one side, so we shall luxuriate in venison while it lasts. We think that Edwards will surely be up to-night, but unless he brings supplies our case is looking serious. The flour is running low, there is only coffee for one week, and I have only a scanty three ounces of tea left. The baking-powder is nearly at an end. We have agreed to economise by breakfasting very late, and having two meals a day instead of three. The young men went out hunting as usual, and I went out and found Birdie, and on her, brought in four other horses, but the snow balled so badly that I went out and walked across the river on a very passable ice bridge, and got some new views of the unique grandeur of this place. Our evenings are social and pleasant. We finish supper about eight, and make up a huge fire. The men smoke

LETTER XV.

A Whisky Slave—The Pleasures of Monotony—The Mountain Lion —" Another Mouth to feed "—A tiresome Boy—An Outcast —Thanksgiving Day—The Newcomer—A Literary Humbug— Milking a dry Cow—Trout-fishing—A Snow-storm—A Desperado's din.

ESTES PARK, *Sunday.*

A TRAPPER passing last night brought us the news that Mr. Nugent is ill; so, after washing up the things after our late breakfast, I rode to his cabin, but I met him in the gulch coming down to see us. He said he had caught cold on the Range, and was suffering from an old arrow wound in the lung. We had a long conversation without adverting to the former one, and he told me some of the present circumstances of his ruined life. It is piteous that a man like him, in the prime of life, should be destitute of home and love, and live a life of darkness in a den with no companions but guilty memories, and a dog which many people think is the nobler animal of the two. I urged him to give up the whisky which at present is his ruin, and his answer had the ring of a sad truth in it: " I cannot, it binds me hand and foot —I cannot give up the only pleasure I have." His ideas of right are the queerest possible. He says that he believes in God, but what he knows or believes of God's law I know not. To resent insult with your revolver, to revenge yourself on those who have injured you, to be true to a comrade and share your last crust with him, to be chivalrous to good women, to be generous and hospitable, and at the last to die game—these are the articles of his creed, and I suppose they are received by men of his stamp. He hates Evans with a bitter hatred, and Evans returns it, having undergone much provocation from Jim in his moods of lawlessness and violence, and being not a little envious of the fascination which his manners and conversation have for the strangers who come up here.

On returning down the gulch the view was grander than I have ever seen it, the gulch in dark shadow, the Park below lying in intense sunlight, with all the majestic canyons which sweep down upon it in depths of infinite blue gloom, and above, the pearly peaks, dazzling in purity and glorious in form, cleft the turquoise blue of the sky. How shall I ever leave this "land which is very far off"? How *can* I ever leave it? is the real question. We are going on the principle, "Let us eat and drink, for to-morrow we die," and the stores are melting away. The two meals are not an economical plan, for we are so much more hungry that we eat more than when we had three.

We had a good deal of sacred music to-day, to make it as like Sunday as possible. The "faint melancholy" of this winter loneliness is very fascinating. How glorious the amber fires of the winter dawns are, and how gloriously to-night the crimson clouds descended just to the mountain-tops and were reflected on the pure surface of the snow! The door of this room looks due north, and as I write the Pole Star blazes, and a cold crescent moon hangs over the ghastliness of Long's Peak.

ESTES PARK, COLORADO, *November.*

We have lost count of time, and can only agree on the fact that the date is somewhere near the end of November. Our life has settled down into serenity, and our singular and enforced partnership is very pleasant. We might be three men living together, but for the unvarying courtesy and consideration which they show to me. Our work goes on like clockwork; the only difficulty which ever arises is that the men do not like me to do anything that they think hard or unsuitable, such as saddling a horse or bringing in water. The days go very fast; it was 3.30 to-day before I knew that it was 1. It is a calm life without worries. The men are so easy to live with; they never fuss, or grumble, or sigh, or make a trouble of anything. It would amuse you to come into our wretched little kitchen before our disgracefully late breakfast, and find Mr. Kavan busy at the stove frying venison, myself washing the supper-dishes, and Mr. Buchan drying them, or both the men busy at the stove while I sweep the floor. Our food is a great object of interest to us, and we are ravenously hungry now that we have only two meals a day. About sundown each goes forth to his "chores"—Mr. K. to chop wood, Mr. B. to haul water, I to wash the milk-pans and water the horses. On Saturday the men shot a deer, and on going for it to-day they found nothing but the hind legs, and following a track which they expected would lead them to a beast's hole, they came quite carelessly upon a large mountain lion, which, however, took itself out of their reach before they were sufficiently recovered from their surprise to fire at it. These lions, which are really a species of puma, are bloodthirsty as well as cowardly. Lately one got into a sheepfold in the canyon of the St. Vrain, and killed thirty sheep, sucking the blood from their throats.

November ?

This has been a day of minor events, as well as a busy one. I was so busy that I never sat down from 10.30 till 1.30. I had washed my one change of raiment, and though I never iron my clothes, I like to bleach them till they are as white as snow, and they were whitening on the line when some furious gusts came down from Long's Peak, against which I could not stand, and when I did get out all my clothes were blown into strips from an inch to four inches in width, literally destroyed! One learns how very little is necessary either for comfort or happiness. I made a four-pound spiced ginger cake, baked some bread, mended my riding dress, cleaned up generally, wrote some letters with the hope that some day they might be posted, and took a magnificent walk, reaching the cabin again in the melancholy glory which now immediately precedes the darkness. We were all busy getting our supper ready when the dogs began to bark furiously, and we heard the noise of horses. "Evans at last!" we exclaimed, but we were wrong. Mr. Kavan went out, and returned saying that it was a young man who had come up with Evans's waggon and team, and that the waggon had gone over into a gulch seven miles from here. Mr. Kavan looked very grave. "It's another mouth to feed," he said. They asked no questions, and brought the lad in, a slangy, assured fellow of twenty, who, having fallen into delicate health at a theological college, had been sent up here by Evans to work for his board. The men were too courteous to ask him what he was doing up here, but I boldly asked him where he lived, and to our dismay he replied, "I've come to live here." So we had to settle what to do with him. We discussed the food question gravely, as it presented a real difficulty. We put him into a bed-closet opening from the kitchen, and decided to see what he was fit for before giving him work. We were very much amazed, in truth, at his coming here. He is evidently a shallow, arrogant youth.

We have decided that to-day is November 26th; to-morrow is Thanksgiving Day, and we are planning a feast, though Mr. K. said to me again this morning, with a doleful face, "You see there's another mouth to feed." This "mouth" has come up to try the panacea of manual labour, but he is town-bred, and I see that he will do nothing. He is writing poetry, and while I was busy to-day began to read it aloud to me, asking for my criticism. He is just at the age when everything literary has a fascination, and every literary person is a hero, specially Dr. Holland. Last night was fearful from the lifting of the cabin and the breaking of the mud from the roof. We sat with fine gravel driving in our faces, and this morning I carried four shovelfuls of mud out of my room. After breakfast, Mr. Kavan, Mr. Lyman, and I, with the two waggon-horses, rode the seven miles to the scene of yesterday's disaster in a perfect gale of wind. I felt like a servant going out for a day's "pleasuring," hurrying "through my dishes," and leaving my room in disorder. The waggon lay half-way down the side of a ravine, kept from destruction by having caught on some trees. It was too cold to hang about while the men hauled it up and fixed it, so I went slowly back, encountering Mr. Nugent in a most bitter mood—almost in an "ugly fit"—hating everybody, and contrasting his own generosity and reckless kindness with the selfishness and carefully-weighed kindnesses of others. People do give him credit for having "as kind a heart as ever beat." Lately a child in the other cabin was taken ill, and though there were idle men and horses at hand, it was only the "desperado" who rode sixty miles in "the shortest time ever made" to bring the doctor. While we were talking he was sitting on a stone outside his den mending a saddle, skins, bones, and skulls lying about him, "Ring" watching him with jealous and idolatrous affection, the wind lifting his thin curls from as grand a head as was ever modelled —a ruin of a man. Yet the sun which shines "on the evil and the good" was lighting up the gold of his hair. May our Father which is in heaven yet show mercy to His outcast child!

Mr. Kavan soon overtook me, and we had an exciting race of two miles, getting home just before the wind fell and the snow began.

Thanksgiving Day. The thing dreaded has come at last, a snowstorm, with a north-east wind. It ceased about midnight, but not till it had covered my bed. Then the mercury fell below zero, and everything froze. I melted a tin of water for washing by

the fire, but it was hard frozen before I could use it.
My hair, which was thoroughly wet with the thawed
snow of yesterday, is hard frozen in plaits. The
milk and treacle are like rock, the eggs have to be
kept on the coolest part of the stove to keep them
fluid. Two calves in the shed were frozen to death.
Half our floor is deep in snow, and it is so cold that
we cannot open the door to shovel it out. The snow
began again at eight this morning, very fine and hard.
It blows in through the chinks and dusts this letter
while I write. Mr. Kavan keeps my ink-bottle close
to the fire, and hands it to me every time that I need
to dip my pen. We have a huge fire, but cannot
raise the temperature above 20°. Ever since I
returned the lake has been hard enough to bear a
waggon, but to-day it is difficult to keep the water-
hole open by the constant use of the axe. The snow
may either melt or block us in. Our only anxiety
is about the supplies. We have tea and coffee enough
to last over to-morrow, the sugar is just done, and the
flour is getting low. It is really serious that we have
" another mouth to feed," and the new-comer is a
ravenous creature, eating more than the three of us.
It dismays me to see his hungry eyes gauging the
supply at breakfast, and to see the loaf disappear.
He told me this morning that he could eat the whole
of what was on the table. He is mad after food, and
I see that Mr. K. is starving himself to make it hold

out. Mr. Buchan is very far from well, and dreads
the prospect of "half rations." All this sounds
laughable, but we shall not laugh if we have to look
hunger in the face! Now in the evening the snow-
clouds, which have blotted out all things, are lifting,
and the winter scene is wonderful. The mercury is
5° below zero, and the aurora is glorious. In my
unchinked room the mercury is 1° below zero. Mr.
Buchan can hardly get his breath; the dryness is
intense. We spent the afternoon cooking the Thanksgiving dinner. I made a wonderful pudding, for
which I had saved eggs and cream for days, and dried
and stoned cherries supplied the place of currants.
I made a bowl of custard for sauce, which the men
said was "splendid ;" also a rolled pudding, with
molasses; and we had venison steaks and potatoes,
but for tea we were obliged to use the tea-leaves of
the morning again. I should think that few people
in America have enjoyed their Thanksgiving dinner
more. We had urged Mr. Nugent to join us; but he
refused, almost savagely, which we regretted. My
four-pound cake made yesterday is all gone! This
wretched boy confesses that he was so hungry in the
night that he got up and ate nearly half of it. He is
trying to cajole me into making another.

November 29.

Before the boy came I had mistaken some faded

cayenne pepper for ginger, and had made a cake with it.   Last evening I put half of it into the cupboard and left the door open.   During the night we heard a commotion in the kitchen and much choking, coughing, and groaning, and at breakfast the boy was unable to swallow food with his usual ravenousness.   After breakfast he came to me whimpering, and asking for something soothing for his throat, admitting that he had seen the " gingerbread," and "felt so starved" in the night that he got up to eat it.   I tried to make him feel that it was " real mean " to eat so much and be so useless, and he said he would do anything to help me, but the men were so "down on him."   I never saw men so patient with a lad before.   He is a most vexing addition to our party, yet one cannot help laughing at him.   He is not honourable, though.   I dare not leave this letter lying on the table, as he would read it.   He writes for two Western periodicals (at least he says so), and he shows us long pieces of his published poetry.   In one there are twenty lines copied (as Mr. Kavan has shown me) without alteration from *Paradise Lost;* in another there are two stanzas from *Resignation,* with only the alteration of " stray " for " dead;" and he has passed the whole of Bonar's *Meeting-place* off as his own.   Again, he lent me an essay by himself, called *The Function of the Novelist,* which is nothing but a mosaic of unacknowledged

quotations. The men tell me that he has " bragged"
to them that on his way here he took shelter in Mr.
Nugent's cabin, found out where he hides his key,
opened his box, and read his letters and MSS. He
is a perfect plague with his ignorance and self-
sufficiency. The first day after he came, while I was
washing up the breakfast-things, he told me that he
intended to do all the dirty work, so I left the knives
and forks in the tub and asked him to wipe and lay
them aside. Two hours afterwards I found them un-
touched. Again, the men went out hunting, and he
said he would chop the wood for several days' use,
and after a few strokes, which were only successful
in chipping off some shavings, he came in and
strummed on the harmonium, leaving me without any
wood with which to make the fire for supper. He
talked about his skill with the lasso, but could not
even catch one of our quietest horses. Worse than
all, he does not know one cow from another. Two
days ago he lost our milch cow in driving her in to
be milked, and Mr. Kavan lost hours of valuable time
in hunting for her without success. To-day he told
us triumphantly that he had found her, and he was
sent out to milk her. After two hours he returned
with a rueful face and a few drops of whitish fluid in
the milk-pail, saying that that was all he could get.
On Mr. K. going out, he found, instead of our " calico "
cow, a brindled one that had been dry since the

spring! Our cow has gone off to the wild cattle, and we are looking very grim at Lyman, who says that he expected he should live on milk. I told him to fill up the four-gallon kettle, and an hour afterwards found it red-hot on the stove. Nothing can be kept from him unless it is hidden in my room. He has eaten two pounds of dried cherries from the shelf, half of my second four-pound spiced loaf before it was cold, licked up my custard sauce in the night, and privately devoured the pudding which was to be for supper. He confesses to it all, and says, "I suppose you think me a cure." Mr. K. says that the first thing he said to him this morning was, "Will Miss B. make us a nice pudding to-day?" This is all harmless, but the plagiarism and want of honour are disgusting, and quite out of keeping with his profession of being a theological student.

This life is in some respects like being on board ship—there are no mails, and one knows nothing beyond one's little world, a very little one in this case. We find each other true, and have learnt to esteem and trust each other. I should, for instance, go out of this room leaving this book open on the table, knowing that the men would not read my letter. They are discreet, reticent, observant, and on many subjects well-informed, but they are of a type which has no antitype at home. All women work in this region, so there is no fuss about my working, or say-

ing, "Oh, you mustn't do that," or "Oh, let me do
that."

November 30.

We sat up till eleven last night, so confident
were we that Edwards would leave Denver the
day after Thanksgiving and get up here.   This
morning we came to the resolution that we must
break up.   Tea, coffee, and sugar are done, the venison is turning sour, and the men have only one month
left for the hunting on which their winter living
depends.   I cannot leave the Territory till I get
money, but I can go to Longmount for the mail and
hear whether the panic is abating.   Yesterday I was
alone all day, and after riding to the base of Long's
Peak, made two roly-poly puddings for supper, having
nothing else.   The men, however, came back perfectly loaded with trout, and we had a feast.   Epicures
at home would have envied us.   Mr. Kavan kept the
frying-pan with boiling butter on the stove, butter
enough thoroughly to cover the trout, rolled them in
coarse corn-meal, plunged them into the butter,
turned them once, and took them out, thoroughly
done, fizzing, and lemon-coloured.   For once young
Lyman was satisfied, for the dish was replenished as
often as it was emptied.   They caught 40 lbs., and
have packed them in ice until they can be sent to
Denver for sale.   The winter fishing is very rich.
In the hardest frost, men who fish not for sport, but

gain, take their axes and camping blankets, and go
up to the hard-frozen waters which lie in fifty places
round the Park, and choosing a likely spot, a little
sheltered from the wind, hack a hole in the ice, and
fastening a foot-link to a cotton-wood tree, bait the
hook with maggots or bits of easily-gotten fresh meat.
Often the trout are caught as fast as the hook can be
baited, and looking through the ice-hole in the track
of a sunbeam, you see a mass of tails, silver fins,
bright eyes, and crimson spots, a perfect shoal of fish,
and truly beautiful the crimson-spotted creatures
look, lying still and dead on the blue ice under the
sunshine. Sometimes two men bring home 60 lbs.
of trout as the result of one day's winter fishing. It
is a cold and silent sport, however. How a cook at
home would despise our scanty appliances, with which
we turn out luxuries. We have only a cooking-
stove, which requires incessant feeding with wood, a
kettle, a frying-pan, a six-gallon brass pan, and a
bottle for a rolling-pin. The cold has been very
severe, but I do not suffer from it even in my
insufficient clothing. I take a piece of granite made
very hot to bed, draw the blankets over my head,
and sleep eight hours, though the snow often covers
me. One day of snow, mist, and darkness was rather
depressing, and yesterday a hurricane began about
five in the morning, and the whole Park was one
swirl of drifting snow, like stinging wood smoke.

My bed and room were white, and the frost was so intense that water brought in a kettle hot from the fire froze as I poured it into the basin. Then the snow ceased, and a fierce wind blew most of it out of the Park, lifting it from the mountains in such clouds as to make Long's Peak look like a smoking volcano. To-day the sky has resumed its delicious blue, and the Park its unrivalled beauty. I have cleaned all the windows, which, ever since I have been here, I supposed were of discoloured glass, so opaque and dirty they were; and when the men came home from fishing they found a cheerful new world. We had a great deal of sacred music and singing on Sunday. Mr. Buchan asked me if I knew a tune called "America," and began the grand roll of our National Anthem to the words:

> "My country, 'tis of thee,
> Sweet land of liberty," etc.

December 1.

I was to have started for Canyon to-day, but was awoke by snow as stinging as pinpoints beating on my hand. We all got up early, but it did not improve until nearly noon. In the afternoon Lyman and I rode to Mr. Nugent's cabin. I wanted him to read and correct my letter to you, giving the account of our ascent of Long's Peak, but he said he could not, and insisted on our going in, for which young Lyman was more anxious than I was, as Mr. Kavan had seen "Jim" in the morning, and departed from his usual reticence so far as to say, "There's something wrong with that man; he'll either shoot himself or somebody else." However, the "ugly fit" had passed off, and he was so very pleasant and courteous that we remained the whole afternoon. Lyman's one thought was that he could make capital out of the interview, and write an account of the celebrated desperado for a Western paper. The interior of the den was frightful, yet among his black and hideous surroundings the grace of his manner and the genius of his conversation were only more apparent. I read my letter aloud —or rather "The Ascent of Long's Peak," which I have written for *Out West*—and was sincerely interested with the taste and acumen of his criticisms on the style. He is a true child of nature; his eye brightened and his whole face became radiant, and at last tears rolled down his cheek when I read the account of the glory of the sunrise. Then he read us a very able paper on Spiritualism which he was writing. The den was dense with smoke, and very dark, littered with hay, old blankets, skins, bones, tins, logs, powder-flasks, magazines, old books, old moccasins, horseshoes, and relics of all kinds. He had no better seat to offer me than a log, but offered it with a graceful unconsciousness that it was any-

thing less luxurious than an easy-chair. Two valuable rifles and a Sharp's revolver hung on the wall,
and the sash and badge of a scout. I could not help
looking at "Jim" as he stood talking to me. He
goes mad with drink at times, swears fearfully, has
an ungovernable temper. He has formerly led a
desperate life, and is at times even now undoubtedly
a ruffian. There is hardly a fireside in Colorado
where fearful stories of him as an Indian fighter are
not told; mothers frighten their naughty children by
telling them that "Mountain Jim" will get them,
and doubtless his faults are glaring, but he is undoubtedly fascinating, and enjoys a popularity or
notoriety which no other person has. He offered to
be my guide to the plains when I go away. Lyman
asked me if I should not be afraid of being murdered,
but one could not be safer than with him I have often
been told.

The cold was truly awful. I had caught a chill
in the morning from putting on my clothes before
they were dry, and the warmth of the smoky den
was most agreeable; but we had a fearful ride back
in the dusk, a gale nearly blowing us off our horses,
drifting snow nearly blinding us, and the mercury
below zero. I felt as if I were going to be laid up
with a severe cold, but the men suggested a trapper's
remedy—a tumbler of hot water, with a pinch of
cayenne pepper in it—which proved a very rapid

cure. They kindly say that if the snow detains me
here they also will remain. They tell me that they
were horrified when I arrived, as they thought that
they could not make me comfortable, and that I had
never been used to do anything for myself, and then
we complimented each other all round. To-morrow,
weather permitting, I set off for a ride of 100 miles,
and my next letter will be my last from the Rocky
Mountains.

I. L. B.

LETTER XVI.

A Harmonious Home—Intense Cold—A Purple Sun—A Grim Jest —A Perilous Ride—Frozen Eyelids—Long Mount—The Pathless Prairie—Hardships of Emigrant Life—A Trapper's Advice The Little Thompson—Evans and Jim.

DR. HUGHES'S, LOWER CANYON, COLORADO, *Dec. 4.*

ONCE again here, in refined and cultured society, with harmonious voices about me, and dear sweet, loving children whose winning ways make this cabin a true English home. "England, with all thy faults, I love thee still!" I can truly say,

> "Where'er I roam, whatever realms I see,
> My heart, untravelled, fondly turns to thee."

If it swerved a little in the Sandwich Islands, it is true to the Pole now! Surely one advantage of travelling is that, while it removes much prejudice against foreigners and their customs, it intensifies tenfold one's appreciation of the good at home, and, above all, of the quietness and purity of English domestic life. These reflections are forced upon me by the sweet child-voices about me, and by the exquisite consideration and tenderness which are the atmosphere (some would call it the hothouse atmosphere) of this house. But with the bare, hard life, and the bare, bleak mountains around, who could find fault with even a hothouse atmosphere, if it can nourish such a flower of Paradise as sacred human love?

The mercury is eleven degrees below zero, and I have to keep my ink on the stove to prevent it from freezing. The cold is intense — a clear, brilliant, stimulating cold, so dry that even in my threadbare flannel riding-dress I do not suffer from it. I must now take up my narrative of the nothings which have all the interest of *somethings* to me. We all got up before daybreak on Tuesday, and breakfasted at seven. I have not seen the dawn for some time, with its amber fires deepening into red, and the snow peaks flushing one by one, and it seemed a new miracle. It was a west wind, and we all thought it promised well. I took only two pounds of luggage, some raisins, the mail bag, and an additional blanket under my saddle. I had not been up from the Park at sunrise before, and it was quite glorious, the purple depths of M'Ginn's Gulch, from which at a height of 9000 feet you look down on the sunlit Park 1500 feet below, lying in a red haze, with its pearly needle-shaped peaks, framed by mountain-sides dark with pines—my glorious, solitary, unique mountain home! The purple sun rose in front. Had

I known what made it purple I should certainly
have gone no farther.   Then clouds, the morning mist
as I supposed, lifted themselves up rose-lighted,
showing the sun's disc as purple as one of the jars
in a chemist's window, and having permitted this
glimpse of their king, came down again as a dense
mist, the wind chopped round, and the mist began
to freeze hard.   Soon Birdie and myself were a mass
of acicular crystals; it was a true easterly fog.   I
galloped on, hoping to get through it, unable to see
a yard before me; but it thickened, and I was
obliged to subside into a jog-trot.   As I rode on,
about four miles from the cabin, a human figure,
looking gigantic like the spectre of the Brocken,
with long hair white as snow, appeared close to me,
and at the same moment there was the flash of a
pistol close to my ear, and I recognised "Mountain
Jim" frozen from head to foot, looking a century old
with his snowy hair.   It was "ugly" altogether
certainly, a "desperado's" grim jest, and it was best
to accept it as such, though I had just cause for
displeasure.   He stormed and scolded, dragged me
off the pony—for my hands and feet were numb
with cold—took the bridle, and went off at a rapid
stride, so that I had to run to keep them in sight in
the darkness, for we were off the road in a thicket of
scrub, looking like white branch-coral, I knew not
where.   Then we came suddenly on his cabin, and

dear old "Ring," white like all else; and the "ruffian" insisted on my going in, and he made a good fire, and heated some coffee, raging all the time. He said everything against my going forward, except that it was dangerous; all he said came true, and here I am safe! Your letters, however, outweighed everything but danger, and I decided on going on, when he said, "I've seen many foolish people, but never one so foolish as you—you haven't a grain of sense. Why, I, an old mountaineer, wouldn't go down to the plains to-day." I told him he could not, though he would like it very much, for that he had turned his horses loose; on which he laughed heartily, and more heartily still at the stories I told him of young Lyman, so that I have still a doubt how much of the dark moods I have lately seen was assumed.

He took me back to the track; and the interview which began with a pistol-shot, ended quite pleasantly. It was an eerie ride, one not to be forgotten, though there was no danger. I could not recognise any localities. Every tree was silvered, and the fir-tree tufts of needles looked like white chrysanthemums. The snow lay a foot deep in the gulches, with its hard, smooth surface marked by the feet of innumerable birds and beasts. Ice bridges had formed across all the streams, and I crossed them without knowing when. Gulches looked fathomless abysses, with clouds boiling up out of them, and shaggy mountain summits, half seen for a moment through the eddies, as quickly vanished. Everything looked vast and indefinite. Then a huge creation, like one of Doré's phantom illustrations, with much breathing of wings, came sailing towards me in a temporary opening in the mist. As with a strange rustle it passed close over my head, I saw, for the first time, the great mountain eagle, carrying a good-sized beast in his talons. It was a noble vision. Then there were ten miles of metamorphosed gulches—silent, awful—many ice bridges, then a frozen drizzle, and then the wind changed from east to north-east. Birdie was covered with exquisite crystals, and her long mane and the long beard which covers her throat were pure white. I saw that I must give up crossing the mountains to this place by an unknown trail; and I struck the old trail to the St. Vrain, which I had never travelled before, but which I knew to be more legible than the new one. The fog grew darker and thicker, the day colder and windier, the drifts deeper; but Birdie, whose four cunning feet had carried me 600 miles, and who in all difficulties proves her value, never flinched or made a false step, or gave me reason to be sorry that I had come on. I got down to the St. Vrain Canyon in good time, and stopped at a house thirteen miles from Longmount to get oats. I was white from head to foot, and my clothes were frozen stiff. The women gave me the usual invitation, "Put your feet in the oven;" and I got my clothes thawed and dried, and a delicious meal consisting of a basin of cream and bread. They said it would be worse on the plains, for it was an easterly storm; but as I was so used to riding, I could get on, so we started at 2.30. Not far off I met Edwards going up at last to Estes Park, and soon after the snowstorm began in earnest—or rather I entered the storm, which had been going on there for several hours. By that time I had reached the prairie, only eight miles from Longmount, and pushed on. It was simply fearful. It was twilight from the thick snow, and I faced a furious east wind loaded with fine, hard-frozen crystals, which literally made my face bleed. I could only see a very short distance anywhere; the drifts were often two feet deep, and only now and then, through the blinding whirl, I caught a glimpse of snow through which withered sunflowers did not protrude, and then I knew that I was on the track. But reaching a wild place, I lost it, and still cantered on, trusting to the pony's sagacity. It failed for once, for she took me on a lake and we fell through the ice into the water, 100 yards from land, and had a hard fight back again. It grew worse and worse. I had wrapped up my face but the sharp, hard snow beat on my eyes—the only exposed part—bringing tears into them, which froze and closed up my eyelids at once. You cannot imagine what that was. I had to take off one glove to pick one eye open, for as to the other, the storm beat so savagely against it that I left it frozen, and drew over it the double piece of flannel which protected my face. I could hardly keep the other open by picking the ice from it constantly with my numb fingers, in doing which I got the back of my hand slightly frostbitten. It was truly awful at the time. I often thought, " Suppose I am going south instead of east? Suppose Birdie should fail? Suppose it should grow quite dark ?" I was mountaineer enough to shake these fears off and keep up my spirits, but I knew how many had perished on the prairie in similar storms. I calculated that if I did not reach Longmount in half an hour it would be quite dark, and that I should be so frozen or paralysed with cold that I should fall off. Not a quarter of an hour after I had wondered how long I could hold on I saw, to my surprise, close to me, half smothered in snow, the scattered houses and blessed lights of Longmount, and welcome, indeed, its wide, dreary, lifeless, soundless road looked ! When I reached the hotel I was so benumbed that I could not get off, and the worthy host lifted me off and carried me in. Not expecting any travellers, they had no fire except in the barroom, so they took me to the stove in their own room, gave me a hot drink and plenty of blankets,

and in half an hour I was all right and ready for a
ferocious meal. "If there's a traveller on the prairie
to-night, God help him!" the host had said to his
wife just before I came in.

I found Evans there, storm-stayed, and that—to
his great credit at the time—my money matters were
all right. After the sound and refreshing sleep which
one gets in this splendid climate, I was ready for an
early start, but, warned by yesterday's experience,
waited till twelve to be sure of the weather. The
air was intensely clear, and the mercury *seventeen
degrees below zero!* The snow sparkled and snapped
under one's feet. It was gloriously beautiful! In
this climate, if you only go out for a short time you
do not feel cold even without a hat, or any additional
wrappings. I bought a cardigan for myself, however, and some thick socks, got some stout snow-
shoes for Birdie's hind feet, had a pleasant talk with
some English friends, did some commissions for the
men in the Park, and hung about waiting for a
freight train to break the track, but eventually, in-
spirited by the good news from you, left Longmount
alone, and for the last time. I little thought that
miserable, broiling day on which I arrived at it with
Dr. and Mrs. Hughes, of the glories of which it was
the gate, and of the "good time" I should have. Now
I am at home in it; every one in it and along the
St. Vrain Canyon addresses me in a friendly way by

name; and the newspapers, with their intolerable personality, have made me and my riding exploits so notorious, that travellers speak courteously to me when they meet me on the prairie, doubtless wishing to see what sort of monster I am! I have met nothing but civility, both of manner and speech, except that distraught pistol-shot. It looked icily beautiful, the snow so pure and the sky such a bright, sharp blue! The snow was so deep and level that after a few miles I left the track, and, steering for Storm Peak, rode sixteen miles over the pathless prairie without seeing man, bird, or beast—a solitude awful even in the bright sunshine. The cold, always great, became piteous. I increased the frostbite of yesterday by exposing my hand in mending the stirrup; and when the sun sank in indescribable beauty behind the mountains, and colour rioted in the sky, I got off and walked the last four miles, and stole in here in the coloured twilight without any one seeing me.

The life of which I wrote before is scarcely less severe, though lightened by a hope of change, and this weather brings out some special severities. The stove has to be in the living-room, the children cannot go out, and, good and delightful as they are, it is hard for them to be shut up all day with four adults. It is more of a trouble than you would think for a lady in precarious health that, before each meal, eggs, butter, milk, preserves, and pickles have to be unfrozen. Unless they are kept on the stove, there is no part of the room in which they do not freeze. It is uninteresting down here in the foothills. I long for the rushing winds, the piled-up peaks, the great pines, the wild night noises, the poetry and the prose of the free, jolly life of my unrivalled eyrie. I can hardly realise that the river which lies ice-bound outside this house is the same which flashes through Estes Park, and which I saw snow-born on Long's Peak.

ESTES PARK, *December 7.*

Yesterday morning the mercury had disappeared, so it was 20° below zero at least. I lay awake from cold all night, but such is the wonderful effect of the climate, that when I got up at half-past five to waken the household for my early start, I felt quite refreshed. We breakfasted on buffalo beef, and I left at eight to ride forty-five miles before night, Dr. Hughes and a gentleman who was staying there convoying me the first fifteen miles. I did like that ride, racing with the other riders, careering through the intoxicating air in that indescribable sunshine, the powdery snow spurned from the horses' feet like dust! I was soon warm. We stopped at a trapper's ranch to feed, and the old trapper amused me by seeming to think Estes Park almost inaccessible in winter. The distance was greater than I had been told, and he said that I could not get there before eleven at night, and not at all if there was much drift. I wanted the gentlemen to go on with me as far as the Devil's Gate, but they could not because their horses were tired; and when the trapper heard that, he exclaimed, indignantly, "What! that woman going into the mountains alone? She'll lose the track or be froze to death!" But when I told him I had ridden the trail in the storm of Tuesday, and had ridden over six hundred miles alone in the mountains, he treated me with great respect as a fellow-mountaineer, and gave me some matches, saying, "You'll have to camp out anyhow; you'd better make a fire than be froze to death." The idea of my spending the night in the forest alone, by a fire, struck me as most grotesque.

We did not start again till one, and the two gentlemen rode the first two miles with me. On that track, the Little Thompson, there a full stream, has to be crossed eighteen times, and they had been hauling wood across it, breaking it, and it had broken and refrozen several times, making thick and thin places—indeed, there were crossings which even I thought bad, where the ice let us through, and it was hard for the horses to struggle upon it again; and one of the gentlemen who, though a most accomplished man, was not a horseman, was once or twice in the ludicrous position of hesitating on the bank with an anxious face, not daring to spur his horse upon the ice. After they left me I had eight more crossings, and then a ride of six miles, before I reached the old trail; but though there were several drifts up to the saddle, and no one had broken a track, Birdie showed such pluck, that instead of spending the night by a camp fire, or not getting in till midnight, I reached Mr. Nugent's cabin, four miles from Estes Park, only an hour after dark, very cold, and with the pony so tired that she could hardly put one foot before another. Indeed, I walked the last three miles. I saw light through the chinks, but, hearing an earnest conversation within, was just about to withdraw, when "Ring" barked, and on his master coming to the door I found that the solitary man was talking to his dog. He was looking out for me, and had some coffee ready, and a large fire, which were very pleasant; and I was very glad to get the latest news from the Park. He said that Evans told him that it would be most difficult for any one of them to take me down to the plains, but that he would go, which is a great relief. According to the Scotch proverb, " Better a finger off than aye wagging," and as I cannot live here (for you would not like the life or climate), the sooner I leave the better.

The solitary ride to Evans's was very eerie. It

was very dark, and the noises were unintelligible. Young Lyman rushed out to take my horse, and the light and warmth within were delightful, but there was a stiffness about the new *régime*.   Evans, though steeped in difficulties, was as hearty and generous as ever ; but Edwards, who had assumed the management, is prudent, if not parsimonious, thinks we wasted the supplies recklessly, and the limitations as to milk, etc., are painfully apparent.   A young ex-Guardsman has come up with Evans, of whom the sanguine creature forms great expectations, to be disappointed doubtless.   In the afternoon of yesterday a gentleman came who I thought was another stranger, strikingly handsome, well-dressed, and barely forty, with sixteen shining gold curls falling down his collar ; he walked in, and it was only after a careful second look that I recognised in our visitor the redoubtable " desperado."   Evans courteously pressed him to stay and dine with us, and not only did he show the most singular conversational dexterity in talking with the stranger, who was a very well-informed man, and had seen a great deal of the world, but, though he lives and eats like a savage, his manners and way of eating were as refined as possible.   I notice that Evans is never quite himself or perfectly comfortable when he is there ; and on the part of the other there is a sort of stiffly-assumed cordiality, significant, I fear, of lurking hatred on

LETTER XVII.

Woman's Mission—The Lost Morning—Crossing the St. Vrain—
  Miller—The St. Vrain again—Crossing the Prairie—Jim's
  Dream—"Keeping Strangers"—The Inn Kitchen—A reputed
  Child-Eater—Notoriety—A quiet Dance—Jim's Resolve—The
  Frost-Fall—An unfortunate Introduction.

CHEYENNE, WYOMING, *December 12.*

THE last evening came.   I did not wish to realise it, as
I looked at the snow-peaks glistening in the moonlight.   No woman will be seen in the Park till next
May.   Young Lyman talked in a "hifalutin" style, but
with some truth in it, of the influence of a woman's
presence, how "low, mean, vulgar talk" had died out
on my return, how they had "all pulled themselves
up," and how Mr. Kavan and Mr. Buchan had said
they would like always to be as quiet and gentlemanly as when a lady was with them.   "By May,"
he said, "we shall be little better than brutes, in our
manners at least."   I have seen a great deal of the
roughest class of men both on sea and land during
the last two years, and the more important I think
the "mission" of every quiet, refined, self-respecting
woman—the more mistaken I think those who would

forfeit it by noisy self-assertion, masculinity, or fast-ness. In all this wild West the influence of woman is second only in its benefits to the influence of reli-gion, and where the last unhappily does not exist the first continually exerts its restraining power. The last morning came. I cleaned up my room and sat at the window watching the red and gold of one of the most glorious of winter sunrises, and the slow lighting-up of one peak after another. I have written that this scenery is not lovable, but I love it.

I left on Birdie at 11 o'clock, Evans riding with me as far as Mr. Nugent's. He was telling me so many things, that at the top of the hill I forgot to turn round and take a last look at my colossal, re-splendent, lonely, sunlit den, but it was needless, for I carry it away with me. I should not have been able to leave if Mr. Nugent had not offered his ser-vices. His chivalry to women is so well known, that Evans said I could be safer and better cared for with no one. He added, "His heart is good and kind, as kind a heart as ever beat. He's a great enemy of his own, but he's been living pretty quietly for the last four years." At the door of his den I took leave of Birdie, who had been my faithful companion for more than 700 miles of travelling, and of Evans, who had been uniformly kind to me and just in all his deal-ings, even to paying to me at that moment the very last dollar he owed me. May God bless him and his!

without prayer—prayer chiefly that God would give him a happy death. He had previously promised that he would not hurry or scold, but "fyking" had not been included in the arrangement, and when in the early darkness we reached the steep hill, at whose foot the rapid deep St. Vrain flows, he "fyked" unreasonably about me, the mare, and the crossing generally, and seemed to think I could not get through, for the ice had been cut with an axe, and we could not see whether "glaze" had formed since or no. I was to have slept at the house of a woman farther down the canyon, who never ceases talking, but Miller, the young man whose attractive house and admirable habits I have mentioned before, came out and said his house was "now fixed for ladies," so we stayed there, and I was "made as comfortable" as could be. His house is a model. He cleans everything as soon as it is used, so nothing is ever dirty, and his stove and cooking gear in their bright parts look like polished silver. It was amusing to hear the two men talk like two women about various ways of making bread and biscuits, one even writing out a recipe for the other. It was almost grievous that a solitary man should have the power of making a house so comfortable! They heated a stone for my feet, warmed a blanket for me to sleep in, and put logs enough on the fire to burn all night, for the mercury was eleven below zero. The stars were in-

tensely bright, and a well-defined auroral arch,
throwing off fantastic coruscations, lighted the whole
northern sky. Yet I was only in the foothills, and
Long's glorious Peak was not to be seen. Miller had
all his things "washed up" and his "pots and pans"
cleaned in ten minutes after supper, and then had the
whole evening in which to smoke and enjoy himself
—a poor woman would probably have been " fussing
round" till 10 o'clock about the same work. Besides
Ring there was another gigantic dog craving for notice,
and two large cats, which, the whole evening, were on
their master's knee. Cold as the night was, the house
was chinked, and the rooms felt quite warm. I even
missed the free currents of air which I had been used
to ! This was my last evening in what may be called
a mountainous region.

The next morning, as soon as the sun was well
risen, we left for our journey of 30 miles, which had
to be done nearly at a foot's pace, owing to one horse
being encumbered with my luggage. I did not wish
to realise that it was my last ride, and my last asso-
ciation with any of the men of the mountains whom
I had learned to trust, and in some respects to admire.
No more hunters' tales told while the pine knots
crack and blaze; no more thrilling narratives of
adventures with Indians and bears; and never again
shall I hear that strange talk of Nature and her
doings which is the speech of those who live with her

and her alone. Already the dismalness of a level land comes over me. The canyon of the St. Vrain was in all its glory of colour, but we had a remarkably ugly crossing of that brilliant river, which was frozen all over, except an unpleasant gap of about two feet in the middle. Mr. Nugent had to drive the frightened horses through, while I, having crossed on some logs lower down, had to catch them on the other side as they plunged to shore trembling with fear. Then we emerged on the vast expanse of the glittering plains, and a sudden sweep of wind made the cold so intolerable that I had to go into a house to get warm. This was the last house we saw till we reached our destination that night. I never saw the mountain range look so beautiful—uplifted in every shade of transparent blue, till the sublimity of Long's Peak, and the lofty crest of Storm Peak, bore only unsullied snow against the sky. Peaks gleamed in living light; canyons lay in depths of purple shade; 100 miles away Pike's Peak rose a lump of blue, and over all, through that glorious afternoon, a veil of blue spiritualised without dimming the outlines of that most glorious range, making it look like the dreamed-of mountains of "the land which is very far off," till at sunset it stood out sharp in glories of violet and opal, and the whole horizon up to a great height was suffused with the deep rose and pure orange of the afterglow. It seemed all dream-like as we passed through the sunlit solitude, on the right the prairie waves lessening towards the far horizon, while on the left they broke in great snowy surges against the Rocky Mountains. All that day we neither saw man, beast, nor bird. "Jim" was silent mostly. Like all true children of the mountains, he pined even when temporarily absent from them.

At sunset we reached a cluster of houses called Namaqua, where, to my dismay, I heard that there was to be a dance at the one little inn to which we were going at St. Louis. I pictured to myself no privacy, no peace, no sleep, drinking, low sounds, and worse than all, "Jim" getting into a quarrel and using his pistols. He was uncomfortable about it for another reason. He said he had dreamt the night before that there was to be a dance, and that he had to shoot a man for making "an unpleasant remark!" For the last three miles which we accomplished after sunset the cold was most severe, but nothing could exceed the beauty of the afterglow, and the strange look of the rolling plains of snow beneath it. When we got to the queer little place where they "keep strangers" at St. Louis, they were very civil, and said that after supper we could have the kitchen to ourselves. I found a large, *prononcée*, competent, bustling widow, hugely stout, able to manage all men and everything else, and a very florid sister like herself, top-heavy with hair. There were besides two naughty children in the kitchen, who cried incessantly, and kept opening and shutting the door. There was no place to sit down but a wooden chair by the side of the kitchen stove, at which supper was being cooked for ten men. The bustle and clatter were indescribable, and the landlady asked innumerable questions, and seemed to fill the whole room. The only expedient for me for the night was to sleep on a shakedown in a very small room occupied by the two women and the children, and even this was not available till midnight, when the dance terminated; and there was no place in which to wash except a bowl in the kitchen. I sat by the stove till supper, wearying of the noise and bustle after the quiet of Estes Park. The landlady asked, with great eagerness, who the gentleman was who was with me, and said that the men outside were saying that they were sure that it was " Rocky Mountain Jim," but she was sure it was not. When I told her that the men were right, she exclaimed, " Do tell! I want to know! that quiet, kind gentleman!" and she said she used to frighten her children when they were naughty by telling them that " he would get them, for he came down from the mountains every week, and took back a child with him to eat!" She was as proud of having him in her house as if he had been the President, and I gained a reflected importance! All the men in the settlement assembled in the front room, hoping he would go and smoke there, and when he remained in the kitchen they came round the window and into the doorway to look at him. The children got on his knee, and, to my great relief, he kept them good and quiet, and let them play with his curls, to the great delight of the two women, who never took their eyes off him. At last the bad-smelling supper was served, and ten silent men came in and gobbled it up, staring steadily at "Jim" as they gobbled. Afterwards, there seemed no hope of quiet, so we went to the post-office, and while waiting for stamps were shown into the prettiest and most ladylike-looking room I have seen in the West, created by a pretty and refined-looking woman. She made an opportunity for asking me if it were true that the gentleman with me was "Mountain Jim," and added that so very gentlemanly a person could not be guilty of the misdeeds attributed to him. When we returned, the kitchen was much quieter. It was cleared by eight, as the landlady promised; we had it to ourselves till twelve, and could scarcely hear the music. It was a most respectable dance, a fortnightly gathering got up by the neighbouring settlers, most of them young married people, and there was no drinking at all. I wrote to you for some time, while Mr. Nugent copied for himself the poems "In the Glen" and the latter half of "The River without a Bridge," which he re-only allowed of one person standing in it at a time, to sleep soundly and dream of "ninety-and-nine just persons who need no repentance." The landlady was quite taken up with her "distinguished guest." "That kind, quiet gentleman, Mountain Jim! Well, I never! he must be a very good man!"

Yesterday morning the mercury was 20° below zero. I think I never saw such a brilliant atmosphere. That curious phenomena called frost-fall was occurring, in which, whatever moisture may exist in the air, somehow aggregates into feathers and fern-leaves, the loveliest of creations, only seen in rarefied air and intense cold. One breath and they vanish. The air was filled with diamond sparks quite intangible. They seemed just glitter and no more. It was still and cloudless, and the shapes of violet mountains were softened by a veil of the tenderest blue. When the Greeley stage-waggon came up, Mr. Fodder, whom I met at Lower Canyon, was on it. He had expressed a great wish to go to Estes Park, and to hunt with "Mountain Jim," if it would be safe to do the latter. He was now dressed in the extreme of English dandyism, and when I introduced them,[1] he put out a small hand cased in a

[1] This was a truly unfortunate introduction. It was the first link in the chain of circumstances which brought about Mr. Nugent's untimely end, and it was at this person's instigation (when overcome by fear) that Evans fired the shot which proved fatal.

perfectly-fitting lemon-coloured kid glove. As the trapper stood there in his grotesque rags and odds and ends of apparel, his gentlemanliness of deportment brought into relief the innate vulgarity of a rich *parvenu*. Mr. Fodder rattled so amusingly as we drove away that I never realised that my Rocky Mountain life was at an end, not even when I saw "Mountain Jim," with his golden hair yellow in the sunshine, slowly leading the beautiful mare over the snowy plains back to Estes Park, equipped with the saddle on which I had ridden 800 miles!

A drive of several hours over the plains brought us to Greeley, and a few hours later, in the far blue distance, the Rocky Mountains, and all that they enclose, went down below the prairie sea.

I. L. B.

THE END.

VIRAGO MODERN CLASSICS
&
CLASSIC NON-FICTION

The first Virago Modern Classic, *Frost in May* by Antonia White, was published in 1978. It launched a list dedicated to the celebration of women writers and to the rediscovery and reprinting of their works. Its aim was, and is, to demonstrate the existence of a female tradition in fiction, and to broaden the sometimes narrow definition of a 'classic' which has often led to the neglect of interesting novels and short stories. Published with new introductions by some of today's best writers, the books are chosen for many reasons: they may be great works of fiction; they may be wonderful period pieces; they may reveal particular aspects of women's lives; they may be classics of comedy or storytelling.

The companion series, Virago Classic Non-Fiction, includes diaries, letters, literary criticism, and biographies – often by and about authors published in the Virago Modern Classics.

'Good news for everyone writing and reading today' – *Hilary Mantel*

'A continuingly magnificent imprint' – *Joanna Trollope*

'The Virago Modern Classics have reshaped literary history and enriched the reading of us all. No library is complete without them' – *Margaret Drabble*